Conflict First Aid

Conflict First Aid

*How to Stop Personality Clashes
and Disputes from Damaging You
or Your Organization*

Nancy Radford

 BUSINESS EXPERT PRESS

First published in 2018 by
Business Expert Press, LLC
222 East 46th Street, New York, NY 10017
www.businessexpertpress.com

ISBN-13: 978-1-63157-973-8 (paperback)
ISBN-13: 978-1-63157-974-5 (e-book)

Business Expert Press Human Resource Management and Organizational Behavior Collection

Collection ISSN: 1946-5637 (print)
Collection ISSN: 1946-5645 (electronic)

Cover and interior design by S4Carlisle Publishing Services
Private Ltd., Chennai, India

First edition: 2018

10 9 8 7 6 5 4 3 2 1

Printed in the United States of America.

Abstract

This book gives practical tips on how to manage disputes and personality clashes before they create major problems for business and relationships. Written in laymen's terms with examples, acronyms, and illustrations, it helps the reader understand the causes of conflict and how it develops and escalates. The author explains the scientific basis for seemingly illogical behavior under stress and in conflict and also offers tips and tools for managing emotions and behaviors in difficult situations.

Guidance is provided on setting and maintaining standards, balancing responsibilities with relationships, and dealing with negative issues before serious damage is done. The book is structured so that it can either be read as a whole or the relevant section accessed in a crisis, with a toolkit of resources at the end. Each chapter ends with questions to check understanding. Full of convenient tools and insights into managing emotions and handling disagreements, it provides a handy resource for managers and employees.

Keywords

boundaries, conflict management, conflict resolution, confrontations, disagreements, discipline, dispute resolution, personality clashes

All photographs and figures in this article are my own work. Quotations are referenced.

Contents

Acknowledgments

I owe a huge debt of gratitude to the many people who have made this book possible. Thank you so much to

- Business Expert Press and S4Carlisle for making things so easy, especially Nigel, Charlene, Rob, and Kiruthigadevi
- Mentors, leading lights and coaches for guidance; especially Anthony Glaister, Aldo Civico, and the many researchers and authors quoted in this book
- Family, friends, and clients for their unswerving faith in me; especially Frances, Sandy, Clare, Martha, Tim, Rob, Pele, Peter, Ute, Diamond Mastermind Group, the Sauers, Morgans, and all those that trusted me to work with them at critical and difficult times in their lives.
- Jody Chrastek, Ann Seibert, and Alisdair Butler for time reviewing and giving great feedback and encouragement.
- My husband, Giles, for his unstinting encouragement, cheerfulness, and steadfast practical support.

Introduction

Pain and conflict have a lot in common—we try and avoid them both. When they occur, we try and get rid of them as soon as possible and we do not like talking about them. Yet, this is not healthy.

We would all like to avoid pain, yet one of the most dreaded diseases of the past was leprosy, where people lost the ability to feel pain. So, they did not pull away from a burning object, did not feel a rat gnawing at their feet, and ignored sores. This led to injuries festering, loss of limbs, disfigurements, and eventually, death.

When we fear conflict or do not know how to handle it, the cost of avoidance can be high. Avoiding conflict results in festering resentments or eventual explosions. Respect and love fade. Or, we pretend there is no conflict, and instead of talking about it, we act it out—we become sarcastic, uncooperative, or devious. The most common way to "avoid conflict" is to talk **about** people, instead of **to** them. Little issues become big ones. Minor grievances chafe and resentment eats away at contentment. We tell ourselves stories where we are the hero, and the other, the unwitting villain. Our flight or fight response switches on without being able to discharge and stress levels rocket. Research links more and more ailments to this constant state of stimulation.

No matter how civilized a society you live in or how calm and zen-like you become, conflict and pain are a part of life. Yet, if we know the causes, understand our responses, and learn appropriate strategies, we can minimize the negative impact of them both.

This book grew out of my vision to create a practical resource that would help people manage conflict positively, wherever possible. This is not a manual for those who want to go into the field professionally, nor can it take the place of training and experience. It is intended to introduce this critical and interesting facet of leadership as well as provide some guidance in difficult situations. Chapter 4 helps you decide whether to get involved. Chapter 8 highlights some problem areas and gives examples.

As in first aid, there are situations where it is best not to intervene, and in others, you need to call in the experts as quickly as possible. Chapter 9 helps you decide whether to wade in or walk on when others are in conflict, and provides some guidelines on when to call external assistance.

Although you may want to go straight to the practical chapters, reading the first two chapters will help you realize why you and others react in unhelpful ways. This knowledge will enhance your understanding of the practical tools and make it easier to adapt them to your particular situation. Chapter 1 covers the causes of conflict, how it escalates, its costs and potential benefits. It gives a brief overview of conflict styles and common theories of conflict management. Chapter 2 explains how conflict and fear of conflict result in illogical and even self-destructive behavior, due to our brains being hijacked by our Flight/Fight/Freeze Response. Chapter 3 gives you six practical ways to pacify this primitive response, and take back control of your hijacked brain. Chapter 4 takes you through the process of deciding whether to act. Chapter 5 helps you prepare for critical discussions that could potentially lead to conflict. Chapter 6 gives guidelines on how to carry out these *crucial conversations* (Patterson, Grenny, et al. 2002). Good communication is vital and Chapter 7 explores essential skills, with exercise and guidance for improving them. Life does not always give us the chance to prepare, and sometimes, conflict ambushes us. Chapter 8 gives examples and suggests some strategies to help you survive these situations. There are also scenarios for you to practice your new skills. Chapter 9 explores why good people do not get on, and what actions others can take to ease the situation. When things go wrong, Chapter 10 suggest how to turn what seem like disasters into opportunities for development and growth. Chapter 11 turns your mind to the future and learning how to avoid being sucked into the conflict whirlpool. Chapter 12 gathers all the tools scattered throughout this book into one place for ease of use in future, with an overview of recommended resources.

I hope this book opens the door to conflict management and encourages you to explore this fascinating and extremely important topic.

CHAPTER 1

Understanding Conflict

Causes, costs, escalation, and theories

What Causes Conflict?

People have different cultures, values, interests, personalities, status, and access to resources. Of course, differences—of themselves—are not necessarily a cause of conflict. They become a source of conflict when people believe they are not respected, valued, or understood.

Christopher Moore (Moore 2003) presents a model which categorizes differences that often result in conflicts. The following table sets them out.

Moore's model is useful for identifying and analyzing multiple causes of conflict, for example, when different cultures or religions clash, such as between Muslims and Christians. This is often intensified by a lack of information, misinformation, or different interpretations of the data and its relevance. Relationships suffer due to miscommunication, negative behavior, and stereotyping. The resulting competition for power or a voice can cause conflicts of interest and result in destructive behavior patterns, unequal power, and authority. A small difference suddenly becomes a cause for war.

The causes Moore sets out are often more obvious in larger or more formal conflicts, such as international conflicts or civil legal cases. It may be harder to define the cause in domestic or workplace conflict using his criteria. Scott provides another, more practical, description of the reasons people disagree (Scott 2008):

Type of difference	Description
Data	Misinformation, lack of information, different interpretations, different views on what is relevant and important
Interest	Competition for resources (actual or perceived), procedural interests, psychological interests
Value	Different criteria for evaluating ideas or behavior, different ways of life, culture, religion, or ideology
Structural	Unequal power and authority, unequal control or distribution Geographical, physical, or environmental factors, time constraints
Relationship	Strong emotions, stereotyping, miscommunication, negative behavior

Figure 1.1 Causes of Conflict (Moore 2003)

Cause	When conflict may arise
Different needs, interests, or values	When any of these are important and incompatible
Poor communication	Misunderstandings about behavior and intent
Lack of information	Inappropriate assumptions, misunderstandings
Power, control, and responsibility problems	Unfairness, competition, confusion about roles
Difficult people and personality clashes	Different styles of working, fear, threat, anger
Lack of trust	When trust is needed to complete tasks or move forward

Figure 1.2 Everyday Causes of Conflict

In real life, the borders blur and overlap, yet being aware of these categories helps us understand the complexities of disagreements. One cause alone may not be enough to cause problems, but when two or more coincide, conflict becomes almost inevitable. Try and spot the causes in the situation described below.

Exercise

Beaver Brothers-Spot the Causes of Conflict

Stanley has worked for Beaver Brothers for many years. His skill at carving is irreplaceable and a major factor in Beaver Brothers' success in selling bespoke kitchens. He likes working on his own, so often stays late or comes in early, depending on how he feels. Geoff, his manager for the last ten years, is relaxed about timekeeping and hierarchy, as long as the work gets done to the standard and quality expected. All the senior craftspeople have traditionally held keys for the workshop.

Geoff retired two weeks ago, and a new manager, Adrian, was brought into the business. Adrian's brief is to improve efficiency and to ensure that Beaver Brothers is compliant with Health and Safety legislation. Adrian feels that lone working with sharp tools is a potential risk to health and safety. He is also worried that there is no record of the number of keys. He decides to put in an alarm and more secure locks.

He posts up a brief memo on the notice board, saying:

From Monday, there will be new locks on the workshop doors. Keys to the main doors will be held by the manager and deputy manager. All staff will need to work between 7:00 p.m. and 5:00 p.m., the hours when managers are on duty. No one will be allowed to work unsupervised.

Stanley read the notice and was extremely upset. He stormed up to Adrian's office and said that he was extremely insulted. Adrian could not understand why, and said that Stanley was being unreasonable and behaving like a child. Adrian said, "Beaver Brothers needs a real shake-up and bringing up to scratch. It's been the tail wagging the dog for too long." Stanley walked out. The next day, Stanley came in late. He was working on a job that was needed the next day, and at 5:00 p.m., was not completed. He said to the deputy manager, "I'll just stay on and finish it, then come in tomorrow early if need be." The deputy said, "Adrian said no late working, so leave it." The next day, Adrian was in at 7:00 a.m., discovered the job was not completed. He called Stanley in and said that he was disappointed that Stanley had come in late and not completed the job. Stanley resigned, and started a claim for constructive dismissal.

Questions

What does Stanley need? What does Adrian need? Would the different needs alone have caused a problem?

Did missing information contribute to the escalation of the situation?

What assumptions did Stanley make about Adrian's reasons?

What do you think Adrian was thinking about Stanley?

Does thinking about the causes suggest ways of resolving the conflict or its negative impact?

When we examine the reasons behind people's behavior, we begin to see how the situation could have been handled better. It is obvious that better communication and understanding could have prevented the conflict. Different views of roles and lack of trust contributed to the negative assumptions. Once the initial communication was misinterpreted, each subsequent incident was interpreted in a negative way. To resolve the conflict at the stage when Stanley resigns is much harder than to address the issue at an earlier stage.

How Conflict Escalates

In most situations, a minor difference does not cause conflict. In circumstances where emotions are strong, consequences are serious, or there are additional stresses, conflict escalates. As with the example of Beaver Brothers, additional causes come into play as the conflict escalates, making things deteriorate rapidly. With each stage in the process, calming the situation becomes more difficult. Figure 1.3 below illustrates how conflict escalates.

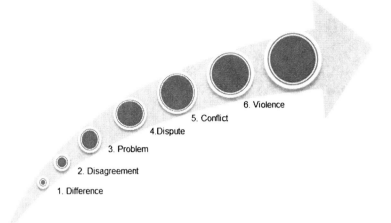

Figure 1.3 How Conflict Escalates

Let us look at each of the stages. **Differences** need not be huge to cause conflict, and they do not necessarily always result in strife. We may enjoy different things, and enhance each other's lives by being different. **Disagreements** occur when people compare and contrast their preferences and priorities. Again, disagreements may have no consequences for us if we agree to disagree. When disagreements or differences cause some negative effects on at least one party, they become perceived as **problems.** In a **dispute**, more than one party is affected, the differences are an issue, and both parties suffer. Any solutions proposed at this stage tend not to consider the other party's interests. **Conflict** is defined as when both parties are engaged in the situation and feel that their goals are incompatible. Both think in terms of "winning" or "not losing." **Violence** refers to either physical or psychological activities that may hurt others. To win, parties take more extreme actions, without caring if they damage or injure each other. In the final stage, **War,** parties seek to destroy the other's power source or even the other party. One or the other may resort to physical violence or litigation. At this stage, the differences that led to this stage may be forgotten, ignored, or distorted. It is now about hurting the other party, even if the action also damages the person taking it.

Practical Example

Escalation of Conflict

Difference: Two of the staff at Tinkers prefer tea and four like coffee.

Disagreement: The fact some like tea and some like coffee is not consequential. Even if they disagree, one person's enjoyment of tea does not hurt those who like coffee.

Problem: The coffee-drinkers decide to spend the staff refreshment budget on a fancy coffee machine. The tea-drinkers are annoyed because the coffee-drinkers have something they do not. They complain to the boss and she points out that there was a vote, and the majority voted for the coffee machine.

Dispute: The tea-drinkers are in charge of arranging the staff social paid for by the company. They arrange for it to be at a caffeine-free tearoom. The coffee-drinkers see this as spite and complain. The tea-drinkers feel that the coffee-drinkers are becoming difficult. Everyone starts to take sides on other issues and find fault with the individuals in the other group. Now, what was a minor issue starts to become unpleasant. Trust has become eroded.

Conflict: The coffee-drinkers refuse to go to the social and say to the boss that they want to have their own event. The boss says that there will not be any event. Both parties blame the other for missing out on an event. The lines are drawn and both feel that their goals are incompatible. They have forgotten it is about tea and coffee and start thinking of **them** and **us.** Actions are misinterpreted; sarcastic comments and fault-finding help each group become more and more entrenched in their view that it is the innocent victim, and the other group, the horrible oppressor.

Violence: The two groups start looking for opportunities to damage each other and disrupt the other's enjoyment of life. They might hide the sugar or put salt in the sugar, or make an official complaint.

War: Now, it is about catching those in the other group doing wrong, spreading rumors, trying to get them sacked. They may come to blows, go to court, or otherwise try to permanently harm each other. The two groups now hate each other and have probably forgotten the cause of the original incident.

The sooner you catch a conflict, the less likely it is to get worse, and the easier it is to minimize damage.

As conflict escalates, misinformation, competition for resources, and power struggles add fuel to the flames. Recognizing differences and disagreements and acknowledging the problems they may cause is essential to managing conflict well. Many feel that to see differences and speak about them causes conflict, yet this silence often causes more problems. When people do not speak about differences, molehills become mountains. If we cannot talk about our different political views, I am more likely to condemn you because I do not understand you. To manage conflict well, we must be open to talking about differences and difficulties in a respectful way.

Costs of Conflict

So, what are the costs of conflict? Although many see it as a win-lose situation, most of the time, if badly handled, it is a lose-lose scenario. Usually, both parties suffer.

Organizational

Unsurprisingly, poorly managed conflicts cost organizations: the average employee spends 2.1 hours a week dealing with conflict. For the United States alone, that translates to 385 million working days spent every year due to conflict in the workplace. (CPP Global Human Capital Report July 2008)

Disagreements and disputes also contribute to poor performance. People focus on grievances and spend time complaining and listening to others complain. Dysfunctional teams pull in different directions.

> Indeed, nearly one in ten even saw it (conflict) lead to a project failure. (CPP Global Human Capital Report July 2008)

Disciplinary and grievance procedures are time- and energy-consuming. If the matter goes to litigation, legal fees mount up. Even if one party wins, it is rare to recover all the costs, never mind the cost of the time spent trying to resolve the conflict.

In addition to the direct costs of legal expenses, insurance costs rise. Theft and sabotage are more likely where there is conflict. Managers spend a considerable amount of time in resolving conflict, damage limitation, and investigations. Staff often leave because of personality clashes or poor working relationships. The cost of recruiting and training new staff is another hidden cost of conflict.

Individual

Conflict also has a negative impact on individuals' health and happiness, with increased rates of both physical and mental illness, leading to absenteeism and loss of morale. Twenty-seven percent of employees have seen conflict lead to personal attacks, and 25 percent have seen it result in sickness or absence. (CPP Global Human Capital Report July 2008)

Disagreements and disputes take an enormous amount of energy and time. Here is an example of how it can impact on businesses and individuals.

Practical Example of Costs of Conflict

Painting Problem

Sylvia had asked Rosie's firm to paint all the corridors in the office block over the weekend so that the work could be done when the offices were empty. When Sylvia came in on Monday morning, one corridor had not been done. All the painting gear had been left in the corridor. She was very upset as some important clients were visiting that day and would be using that corridor. Sylvia did not wait until she got in to her office, but rang Rosie straightaway to ask what was happening. Rosie was not in, so Sylvia left an angry message on her answerphone. Sylvia was so upset and stressed that she snapped at her PA. The PA was hurt as she was just going to suggest a solution, but as Sylvia was horrible to her, she did not bother. Sylvia blamed Rosie for making her annoyed.

Meanwhile, Rosie had picked up the angry message. Rosie was furious as the reason they had not finished the corridor was because Sylvia had said that she had enough paint to do all the job, but this was not the case. Rosie had tried to contact Sylvia without success over the weekend and had left a note on her desk to say the painters would be in once they had bought more paint. Rosie did not stop to think that Sylvia might not have seen her note. She dashed off an angry e-mail and was so upset that she had to go for a walk to calm down before getting down to work. She decided not to bother going to Sylvia's office because of her attitude. When Sylvia got Rosie's e-mail, she was livid.

Soon, there was a flood of angry e-mails and texts flying back and forth. Both became stressed and angry, and this spilled over into their work and private lives.

Sylvia spent the first few minutes with the important clients complaining about the terrible painters. The clients thought she was unprofessional and not focused on their needs, so decide not to use her firm. Sylvia blamed Rosie for this and decided to consult a lawyer to see if she could sue. Her PA went home and complained to her mother about her terrible boss and started looking for a new job.

Rosie was so upset that she went home and complained to her husband all evening. He got so fed up that he asked her why she carried on with customers like that—and she decided that she would not do any more work for Sylvia. Rosie felt so upset about everything that her ulcer started playing up. She could not focus on the estimates she needed to that evening, so lost a job by not getting the estimate in on time.

Neither was aware of the work that was not getting done, the reason for their headaches, or how easily the initial problem could have been sorted.

Both individuals and companies suffered. Time was lost, relationships damaged, and business disrupted. This is such a common phenomenon that people tend to put up with it. Yet, there are ways that either or both the parties could have resolved this situation at various stages. (See Sample Resolutions, p 2 in Chapter 6)

Suppressed Conflict

So, is the answer to suppress conflict and compromise? Sometimes, this can help, but if there is a real problem, refusing to address it usually exacerbates the situation.

If people are frightened of speaking up, it can have serious consequences. If employees do not feel able to speak up about health and safety, accidents are much more likely. If customer complaints are not handled well, businesses lose customers. Unresolved personality clashes cause employees to leave. If employees are unhappy but cannot express themselves, they might go off sick, resign, or even resort to theft or sabotage.

A study of hospitals in 2005 (Silence Kills 2005) found that

Eighty-four percent of healthcare professionals observe colleagues take dangerous shortcuts when working with patients and yet less than ten percent speak up about their concerns.

Another study summarizes it by saying

In this day and age of tight margins, reducing operating costs through better management of conflict is a path more and more of the best companies are taking. It is ironic that many executives still hesitate to invest time and money in improving their employees' conflict management resiliency when the net added value to the company's bottom line can be documented. (John Ford & Associates. 2007)

Benefits of Positive Conflict

Conflict, like pain, is inevitable. And though we often try and avoid both, both are essential to our safety and development. Pain and conflict can confer benefits in the long term if their lessons are learned. As the earlier example of leprosy showed, pain, like conflict, alerts us to situations where we need to act.

Investigations of the reasons for pain or conflict often uncovers something unpleasant and the discovery process itself can be painful. My friend hates going to the dentist, so put off visiting for years, despite niggling pains. Eventually, she was in so much pain from an abscess that she went. Of course, she now had a much larger problem and it was more difficult, expensive, and painful. In the workplace, people pretend things are okay, because they fear raising issues will uncover more problems.

Lack of skills and knowledge stops people exploring the situation and possible solutions. Knowing that a headache may be caused by dehydration, we acknowledge our headache and drink water. If we know what causes the disagreement, why humans react the way they do and how to manage conflict, we are more likely to address it and have a positive result. Conflict is uncomfortable and unpleasant, but out of conflict can come new ideas and creativity.

If we are never challenged, we never learn the value of our beliefs nor do we see how they may be holding us back. Conflict can spur us on when we might have sat in a rut for ages.

> Conflict is the gadfly of thought. It stirs us to observation and memory. It instigates to invention. It shocks us out of sheep-like passivity, and sets us at noting and contriving.
>
> John Dewey

Decision Making and Conflict Styles

There are various ways people manage conflict. Our preferred decision-making styles, which are based on our experience and personalities, vary under stress or in different situations. There is no one ideal decision-making style nor is there a single best way to manage conflict. Understanding the different styles, and when to use them, helps us reduce the risk of unnecessary conflict when managing differences and helps us handle any inevitable conflict better.

One of the most commonly used models of conflict styles is the Thomas-Kilmann Conflict Mode Instrument, shown below in Figure 1.4. Thomas and Kilmann based their model on the assumption that the root of all conflict is the incompatibility between the concerns of two or more parties. The way we handle conflict depends on two factors. First, the degree to which we attempt to satisfy our own concerns, and second, the extent to which we try to meet others' concerns. Thomas and Kilmann name these assertiveness and cooperation. If you are more assertive, you tend to be more proactive and move toward engaging. If you are more cooperative, you put a higher value on others' concerns.

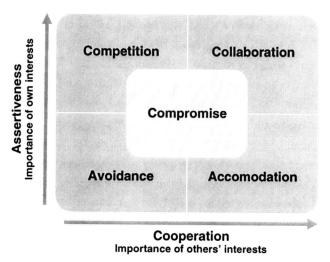

Figure 1.4 Conflict Styles as per Thomas-Kilmann Conflict Mode Instrument

Another widely accepted way of describing the two factors is as the importance of the goal versus the relationship. This is often combined with using animals to illustrate the different styles, as in Figure 1.5 below.

Figure 1.5 Conflict Styles as Animals

Competition (Shark)

This style is characterized by an assertive manner and a strong drive to fulfil the goal. Just as a shark can sense blood at a distance, and zero in for the kill, so this style concentrates on getting the job done. In this style, the goal is more important than relationships. It can be viewed positively as single-minded and focused. In situations where a decision needs to be made quickly, and relationships are not as important as the objective, this style works well. For example, an expert in a medical emergency needs to ensure that the correct treatment is given as swiftly as possible to ensure the survival of the patient. We often revert to this style when frightened or angry, as in a physically dangerous situation, it seems to offer the best chance of survival if you have more power than others (see Chapter 2). It is effective if you are in a position of power, do not need to be concerned about the interests of others, know that your way is the right approach, and time is of the essence. Negatively, it may be seen as self-centered or egotistical and carries a high risk of damaging relationships. This approach may alienate people, and they may withdraw or fight back.

Avoidance (Tortoise)

This style is characterized by less motivation to achieve the goal and a reluctance to engage. Just as a tortoise withdraws into its shell when danger threatens, so this style focuses on withdrawing or ignoring conflict. This, again, is a style that people revert to when under stress and is an instinctive response when one feels powerless (see also Chapter 2). Sometimes, it is the best option. For example, if the issue does not matter to you, you do not have any power to affect the outcome or when you want more time to consider the options. Sometimes, things do resolve themselves if they are ignored. Other times, avoidance can make the situation worse (see Chapter 4 for guidelines on whether to address the situation or not).

Accommodation (Teddy)

This style is characterized by a high level of concern for relationships and less emphasis on achieving one's own objectives. Again, this is an instinctive reaction that we learn from a young age to meet our needs. The teddy is symbolic of the approach a child might take. Without the power to force people to meet his needs, he tries to please them so that his needs are met as a reward. The best times to use this approach are when you want to keep the peace and do not really mind about the outcome, when you recognize that you do not have much power or when the relationship is more important than the goal. This approach does not work well with people who do not care about you or in situations where you have a great deal at stake. Teddies often do not state their own needs clearly and put others first. In some situations, this will result in them being oppressed.

Collaboration (Owl)

This style is characterized by a proactive approach and a strong desire to include others in decision making. The owl symbolizes a consultative approach where everyone's needs and desires are considered, and any action needs to be approved by all parties. This is when you get actively involved in trying to achieve both your own goals and those of the others involved. Often mooted as the ideal approach, as it is called Win-Win, it is not always feasible in reality. It takes willingness and trust on all sides, time is needed to fully explore everyone's needs, resources, and possibilities. When the outcome and relationships are equally important, and there is the time and will to engage fully in the process, this can lead to long-lasting resolutions. However, if there is a lack of trust, time, or willingness to work together, this approach will not work.

Compromise (Fox)

This style uses some elements of all the others. You give up a bit of what you would like to get the rest of what you want and everyone in the conflict does the same. Just as a fox is symbolic of finding an innovative way of getting what he wants, this style looks at the conflict from a different angle. Although this seems like collaboration, it is less time-consuming as it does not necessarily address all needs and issues, but just those needed to resolve the conflict. This will often involve the use of an impartial third party, such as a mediator. At the start of a mediation, I often say that a successful mediation is when both parties are slightly unhappy at having to give up something and happier because they have resolved the issue. This style is useful if neither party is dominant and they have mutually exclusive goals, when a quick resolution is important, when both parties are willing to modify their objectives, and where an agreement of some sort is better than conflict. Compromise is often seen as undesirable or dishonest. However, if people are honest about their needs and priorities, it can be the most practical and beneficial solution. The example below is often used to illustrate a compromise where both parties get what they want, but not what they asked for.

Practical Example of Compromise

The Orange Saga

Jenny, the manager of Le Superior walks into the kitchen to discover Chef Isobel and Chef Michelle arguing over the oranges which have just been delivered. Both chefs are becoming irate and emotional, threatening to walk out if they do not get the oranges. They do not like each other and constantly compete for praise and glory. Isobel says she needs all the oranges for the starter she is making, while Michelle insists that she needs all of them for the wonderful pudding she is preparing. Neither is prepared to change their choice of recipe or to adapt it in any way. If Jenny gives the oranges to either chef, there will be repercussions for days. The problem needs to be sorted as soon as possible as time is ticking away. Menus have been printed and customers will soon be arriving.

Jenny asks to see the recipes. She discovers that Michelle needs the zest of the orange for her orange and ginger cake, whereas Isobel needs the juice for her carrot and orange soup. Jenny says that Michelle is to zest the oranges, and then, give them to Isobel to juice. Neither chef is entirely happy as they did not "win," but they have both saved face and are able to make the chosen recipes.

Roles in Conflict

Just as we have different styles of conflict, we may find ourselves playing a role in the drama that is conflict. Thomas Karpman studied how we tend to manage conflict by taking on either the role of the persecutor, the victim, or the rescuer. Karpman called it a drama triangle, rather than a conflict triangle, because the role is chosen by the individual or projected on to others, rather than a reflection of reality. The Victims in his model are not necessarily victims in real life, but portray themselves as unable to act, oppressed, helpless, or powerless. For this image to work, a Victim needs to find a Perpetrator whom he/she can blame for his/her misfortunes and a Hero to rescue him/her. The presence of the Rescuer gives the Victim the excuse to fail—it is not his/her fault, as the Rescuer should have saved him/her. The Victim does not need to act and does not accept any responsibility.

Those who choose the role of the Rescuer want to help because then, they do not need to tackle their own issues, but can lose themselves in the problems of others. Helping means that they are not a victim or a perpetrator, and they feel morally superior to both. Karman sees rescuers as enablers, whose primary motivator is avoidance of their own problems disguised as concern for others. The victim is confirmed in their impotent role, and the persecutor is damned.

Persecutors blame others for their problems, and may be controlling, blaming, rigid, oppressive, or authoritarian.

Roles are not constant. For example, victims may turn into persecutors when blaming others for their problems. Bullies often have been bullied themselves. Rescuers may become persecutors of the persecutors! Rescuers may even turn on victims who are not grateful or reject their advice. Persecutors may see themselves as victims. This fluid and confusing interplay of roles is most common when emotions and stakes are high. It is helpful to keep this model in mind and to avoid taking on any of the three roles.

Summary of Key Theories of Conflict Management

The recommendations and suggestions which follow are based on extensive reading and research, and tested in my own experience as mediator and conflict coach. There are many excellent books, studies, and online resources on conflict management (see Chapter 12). I will briefly outline here some of the key influences on my practice.

Crucial Conversations (Patterson, Grenny, et al. 2002) is one of the most useful and life-enhancing books that I have read. The team of researchers who wrote it studied interactions and effectiveness of managers in a wide range of situations. They found that the most influential and effective people were those that mastered the art of dialogue. In the book, they studied and identified seven key skills, which could be learned easily, but were transformative. These are called Start with the Heart, Learn to Look, Make it Safe, Master My Stories, State My Path, Explore Others Paths, and Moving to Action. This approach underpins many of the recommendations in this book.

Non-violent Communication (Rosenberg 2015) is another key book. Instead of dialogue, Rosenberg talks about using "Nonviolent Communication" to ensure that we communicate effectively what we feel and need and empathically hear what others feel and need. The table in Figure 1.6 summarizes the theory of nonviolent communication.

Clearly Expressing My View (without blaming or criticizing, speaking in a way which helps you listen)	Empathically Receiving Your View (showing that I am listening without hearing blame or criticism)
Observing what does or does not benefit me and stating it objectively	Listening so that I can accurately reflect back what does not benefit you
Saying how I feel in relation to what I observe (not thoughts, but emotions)	Suspending judgment so that I can understand your feelings
Stating what I need or value that causes my feelings	Clarifying what you need and value that causes your feelings
Clearly requesting that which would benefit me **without demanding.** Suggesting concrete actions that I would like taken "*Would you be willing to. . .?*"	Empathically hearing what you want without feeling demand or resentment, asking or offering something specific "*Would you like me to. . .?*"

Figure 1.6 Non-Violent Communication (Rosenberg 2015)

Another useful book is Scott's *Disagreements, Disputes and All-Out War* (Scott 2008). Scott believes, as I do, that successful management of conflict depends on managing one's own emotions. She believes that there are three simple steps to managing any conflict, which she abbreviates as E.R.I (Emotions, Reason, and Intuition). While I agree with her on the need to bring emotions under control and use reason, I believe that one also needs to learn certain key skills, as advocated by the *Crucial Conversations* team and *Non-violent Communications*.

Even the most skilled mediator or peacemaker can revert to a rampaging warrior in certain circumstances. In Chapter 2, I will explain why this is the case, and in Chapter 3, what we can do about it.

Check Understanding Chapter 1

- Name some causes of conflict.
- What are some of the costs of conflict?
- Is it possible to avoid conflict?
- Are there any benefits of conflict?
- What is your conflict management style at work? At home? Are you happy with how you manage conflict?
- Describe a situation that is an example of Karpman's Drama Triangle.

CHAPTER 2

Brain Hijack

How the evolutionary flight/fight response hijacks the logical brain

Thousands of years of evolution hardwired the flight or fight response into humans. When danger threatens in a primitive world, it is usually a physical danger—a rival warrior, a predator, or a dangerous precipice. To survive these dangers, one had to be swift, strong, or hidden. Those who survived did so by fighting, fleeing, or freezing; these are the genes that we all have inherited. A little bit of neuroscience will help us understand why many people resort to primitive behavior under pressure. Understanding is the first step to controlling the situation and helps us find solutions.

Simplified Neuroscience

Human brains are very complex, yet the simplified diagram in Figure 2.1, illustrating the main functions of the brain, is sufficient for understanding how the flight/fight/freeze response affects our thinking.

The unconscious or reptile brain handles the mechanics of living. The primitive or chimp brain (Peters 2011) is the source of protective instincts and emotions such as anger and fear, which help us survive. The upper-level brain provides wisdom, logic, analysis, compassion, under-standing, and so forth—the thoughts that make us civilized. Figure 2.2 shows what happens when the Flight/Fight/Freeze Instinct is triggered.

The flight/fight/freeze response switches off the logical part of the brain, leaving the primitive brain in control. Evolution hardwired this response into humans as well as other animals because in a physically dangerous world, it helps us survive. In the modern world, the threats and challenges

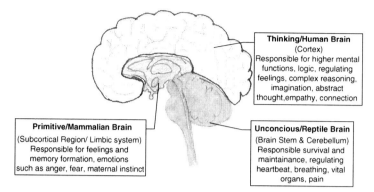

	Thinking/Human Brain (Cortex) Responsible for higher mental functions, logic, regulating feelings, complex reasoning, imagination, abstract thought, empathy, connection
Primitive/Mammalian Brain (Subcortical Region/ Limbic system) Responsible for feelings and memory formation, emotions such as anger, fear, maternal instinct	**Unconcious/Reptile Brain** (Brain Stem & Cerebellum) Responsible survival and maintainance, regulating heartbeat, breathing, vital organs, pain

Figure 2.1 Simplified Cross-section of Human Brain Showing Different Functions

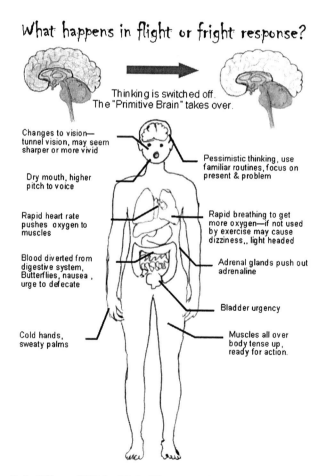

Figure 2.2 Effect of Flight/Fight/Freeze on Human

we face require logic and cooler heads. However, our brains and bodies still react instinctively to threat and competition with this response. Therefore, when we really, really need to say the right thing, we say the wrong one.

Being aware of how evolution hijacks our brains when we are angry or frightened helps us manage our behavior and comprehend that of others.

Negative Spiral

As one can see from Figure 2.2, we think and perceive differently when we are in the grip of the flight/fight/freeze reaction. We see dangers and threats. We interpret others' behavior in negative ways, so become more angry or frightened. The same thing is happening to the others involved in the situation. Logic seems to fly out the window when tempers flare and minor issues can cause major upsets. We get trapped in a negative downward spiral that I call the conflict whirlpool. An example of this is given in the scenario below.

Practical Example

Meat Eater and Vegetarian

Fred and John work together. Fred loves gardening, is a vegetarian, and keen on animal rights. John likes hunting, eats meat, and is keen on socializing and having parties. They work together and get on fairly well. The fact that John and Fred have different interests in life, such as gardening or parties, is not consequential. Even if they disagree on less trivial matters, they can still agree to disagree.

John comes in late and Fred makes a sarcastic comment about how John's socializing seems to be more important to him than work. John feels threatened and says, "Well at least I haven't been off sick as much as you. Maybe you should start eating meat and get stronger."

They both feel upset and angry that their way of life has been challenged. Fred is annoyed and reports John's lateness to the supervisor. John arranges the catering for a meeting and forgets to order vegetarian food. Fred thinks he has done this on purpose and reports him to the supervisor again. John starts looking for a chance to get back at Fred. Their focus has changed from working to complaining about each other and finding fault.

Thought Cycle and Conflict

We do not often realize that we have a choice of response because our brains see behavior, interpret it, and decide on a course of action extremely quickly. Figure 2.3 shows how our minds work when an unexpected event occurs.

One can intervene at any stage of this cycle to change the outcome. The first step is to be aware that we have a choice.

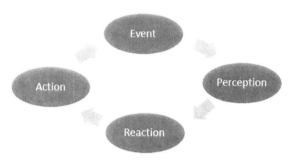

Figure 2.3 Thought Cycle

Between stimulus and response is the freedom to choose. Viktor Frankl

Action

When an unexpected change occurs, the instinctive action is to get mad, back off, or ignore the event. We do not realize that we have perceived it as a threat, reacted, and then, acted based on whether our reaction was flight, fight, or freeze.

If it is important and needs appropriate action which is not physical, the likelihood of getting it wrong when you are not thinking is high. It may start a vicious downward spiral, as in the earlier example.

Medical research has discovered that continuously pumping out adrenalin and cortisone makes us ill and we take longer to recover. Because we do not really think about the situation and the part we play, we keep making the same mistakes. Sometimes, we can control the action, but as we saw, suppressing the outlet can worsen the reaction.

Reaction

We often catch ourselves before the action and are left with the pent-up fear or anger. There are healthy and unhealthy ways of treating stress/ anger/anxiety. Pills, or alcohol, or denial provide some temporary relief. Deep breathing will slow and steady the heart rate, exercise will relieve some tensions and create your own internal opiates. Laughter boosts the immune system and releases pent-up emotions. Various therapies may relieve symptoms. The following chapters contain tools and ideas that will help you to control and manage your reaction.

Perception

You can also change the story you tell yourself about what has happened—however, if you are deep in the flight/fright/freeze response, you may need to calm the reaction first. Changing your perception of an event is more difficult but creates a longer lasting resolution.

Understanding this cycle helps us see that we can intervene at various points, depending how much we are in control. This will help us to choose the most appropriate way to manage our emotions.

Event

And, of course, we could prevent the event occurring. Although, as the Chinese proverb says,

It is better to wear shoes than to try and make the whole world smooth.

Chapter 3 will give you some practical ways to help control your emotions and avoid a brain hijack.

Check Understanding Chapter 2

- Why is evolution important to understanding conflict?
- Why do we often behave illogically under stress?

- What are the benefits and drawbacks of the flight/fight/freeze response?
- What is the first symptom you personally feel when the flight/fight/freeze instinct kicks in?
- Do you have any good strategies for staying calm under stress?
- Describe a situation where the flight/fight/freeze caused you to act in an unhelpful way.

CHAPTER 3

Control Your Emotions

Some practical tools to help you avoid brain hijack

This chapter provides some practical tools to help you act professionally in stressful or conflict situations by managing your emotions. The six key ways to manage emotions presented in this chapter (Pause, Prepare, Posture, Positivity, Practice, and Persistence) are based on psychological and behavioral science research.

The six ways are presented in Figure 3.1 as six peas, as many people find linking an image with an idea embeds it more firmly. The picture can act as a reminder to use the tools.

I have adapted the tools to be easily remembered and practical for everyday use. Where there is conflicting or inconclusive research evidence, such as for posture, I make this clear. With all the tools, it is best to try them out on small annoyances and irritations first to build up skills. **Pause** should be your starting point.

Pause

> Between stimulus and response there is a space. In that space is our power to choose our response. In our response lies our growth and our freedom.

(Frankl 1962)

How often have you heard someone say, "I couldn't help it, he made me angry?" Yet, as we saw from Figure 2.3, it is our thoughts that drive our

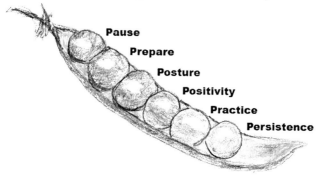

Six Peas to Pacify a Primitive Response

Pause
Prepare
Posture
Positivity
Practice
Persistence

Figure 3.1 The Six Peas: Ways to Control Emotions

reactions and actions, not others. The first instinctive response can be recognized and controlled.

Neuroscientist Jill Bolte Taylor discovered that in 90 seconds, the chemical component of the flight/fright/freeze response is completely dissipated from the blood. She said that if we remain angry or frightened after that initial surge, it is because we choose to do so (Taylor 2006).

Pausing, even for two or three breaths, will help you control your temper and your fear. It gives you the space to assess whether your first interpretation is correct, what the consequences might be, and switch off the primitive flight/fight/freeze response if it is inappropriate.

Pause Tool

When something upsetting happens:

Pause and reflect, if only for an instant. You may want to ask for more time.

Ask yourself

Is my instinctive response keeping me safe from physical danger? (If so, let the primitive brain take over. If not, continue)

Take some deep slow breaths. This will calm and strengthen your heart beat and clear your mind.

Notice how you feel

Ask yourself

> What actually happened?
> What did I tell myself it meant?
> What is another explanation for what happened?

Choose how you want to react.

Taking a few slow deep breaths triggers the vagal nerve, which slows and steadies your heart rate. This reduces the effect of the flight/fight/freeze response. Pausing is an extremely powerful tool. It helps you regain control of your emotions, as well as allows time for you to assess the situation. It also gives those around the impression that you are in control and considering the options. Calm, like fear, is contagious.

> And we have complete control over our own attitude. We are the ones we decide how we feel, how we look at things, how we react.
> Catherine Pulsifer

Prepare

Know Yourself

If we know ourselves, our values, strengths, and our priorities, the way forward becomes clearer. Understanding our natural reactions to conflict help us manage ourselves and the situation better.

Strengths

Knowing our strengths helps us prepare strategies that work for us, not just in conflict, but also in achieving goals. Why not take the online VIA survey (VIA Institute on Character n.d.) to discover your strengths? This will help you work out what inner resources you can call on in conflict. For example, one of my strengths is kindness. Because it is part of my nature, it is easier for me to use compassion to soothe any anger or irritation I may feel toward others. If I remind myself of the pain others are going through, I am less likely to feel anger. Being kind can also calm others and reduce their fears and anger. Small kindnesses such as bringing biscuits to a meeting can ease the atmosphere, and feels natural for me. Another mediator colleague uses his curiosity to engage people, another uses a sense of humor. Knowing your strengths will give you confidence.

Triggers

In *Crucial Conversations* (Patterson, Grenny, et al. 2002), the authors recommend that we look at our own behavior objectively and scientifically.

You feel most powerless when you are least prepared for the worst.

Joseph Grenny

This will help identify patterns, making us aware of any triggers that might set off an unwanted reaction. Be aware of your existing prejudices and perceptions of the situation and the individuals concerned.

Considerations

Identify (beforehand if you have time, or after a situation to learn lessons)

1. What is important
2. The problem—is it an act, pattern or relationship
3. The ideal result
4. What alternatives there are
5. The consequences of handling it badly

Thinking through these issues in advance will help you stay focused. Reviewing past situations with these questions in mind provides valuable lessons for the future.

Review Options

You may find that your response to conflict is shaped by your experience or your training. Review the information on conflict styles in Chapter 1. Spend some time thinking about whether this works for you in all situations. Observe how others handle situations and think about whether this might work for you.

Practical Issues

Practical preparations such as making sure you have all the information, looking at the situation from different angles, or even writing down the main points will help you. Simple things such as being appropriately dressed, allowing plenty of time, and keeping your blood sugar level stable will give you added confidence. Hunger makes most people irritable and carbohydrates can have a calming effect. On the contrary, overeating can also cause problems. Make sure you get plenty of sleep, as lack of sleep causes irritability and irrationality.

> You have power over your mind - not outside events. Realize this, and you will find strength.
>
> Marcus Aurelius

Posture

Most of us are aware of how body language conveys our thoughts and feelings to others, but have you ever considered that changing your posture might make you more courageous and confident in stressful situations?

Stress Hormones

Tens of millions viewed a TED talk on Power Posing by Amy Cuddy (Cuddy 2012), an associate professor at Harvard. This referred to her research (Carney, Cuddy and Yap 2010) on how posture changes our brain chemistry. The effect of posture on stress hormones was then challenged by one of her co-researchers (D. Carney 2015). Carney's position was backed up by later research (Ranehill, et al. 2015); however, this study also found that power posing had a significant effect on self-reported feelings of power. Although there may be no measurable difference in the stress hormones, other therapists and scientists have found that posture can affect perception and mood.

Power of Perception

If you feel more powerful, you will feel less threatened. If you act as if you were calm, it often calms you. Calm, like hysteria, is contagious. There is certainly anecdotal evidence that posture can affect your mood and your perception of yourself, so why not give it a try?

Here are a few suggestions (some you might want to try out in private).

Posture for Confidence

For the Brave: Wonder Woman Pose. Find somewhere unobserved and stand straight, shoulders back, hands on hips, and legs apart for two minutes. (When I demonstrated this to school staff, they said "Ah, the teacher pose.") If done when others are around, it may seem arrogant or threatening, so use with caution.

For the Not So Brave: Straighten. Sit up straight, rest your hands open on your knees or desk, uncross your legs, and put feet firmly on the ground. Bessel van der Kolk describes this as a position in which it is impossible to be angry. (Kolk 2017)

Tilting your head slightly forward deepens and slows your voice. Simon Raybould produced a series of videos (Raybould 2015), demonstrating different postures which make you look and feel more confident.

For Calming and Soothing Fear

Bessel van der Kolk, who helps people with trauma and Post Traumatic Stress Disorder (PTSD), found that certain positions reduced the capacity to feel anger or fear. (Kolk 2017) He found that if people were frozen into positions of fear or terror, they could not feel positive emotions. Conversely, if they sat in what he describes as "The Position of Joy," they were less able to feel fear and anger.

Position of Joy

Sit comfortably with your feet touching the floor and your spine straight.

Rest your hands on your thighs with your palms pointing upward and your fingers gently curved.

Relax your shoulders.

Raise your head.

Take a few slow, deep breaths.

Let go of your anger and fear.

Dr Peter Levine, who works with patients with PTSD describes two techniques which help soothe most people, even those with high levels of anxiety. (Levine 2017)

Posture for Soothing 1: Settling the Body

Sit comfortably with your feet touching the floor and your spine straight.

Put your right hand under your left armpit, with your palm facing inward, beside your heart.

Wrap your left arm around the front of your body so that your left palm touches your upper right arm or shoulder.

Hold yourself gently and firmly in this position, breathing slowly and deeply.

Be aware of the sensation, not just of your hands, but also of your inner body sensations.

Most people report a feeling of settling and safety.

Breathe slowly and deeply, until you feel more settled and calm.

Levine believes this helps people feel that they can contain their feelings. Once the body is more settled, Dr Levine suggests that the following exercise could be tried to further settle the mind and soothe panic, if needed.

Posture for Soothing 2: Settling the Mind and Body

Sit comfortably with your feet touching the floor and your spine straight.

Place the palm of one hand on your forehead, and the palm of your other had on your upper chest.

This can be done with eyes open or closed, whichever must

Breathe slowly and deeply, noticing the sensations of your hands and in your head between your hands.

Leave your hands there until you feel some shift or flow.

Once you feel this, leaving the lower hand on your chest, move the upper hand to your belly.

Breathe slowly and deeply, noticing the sensations in your body between your hands.

Leave your hands there until you feel some shift or flow.

Distancing

Tammy Lenski (Lenski n.d.) writes of the benefits of distance for keeping yourself calm. One way of doing this is to lean back in your chair, physically distancing yourself from the problem. This is a risky strategy to use in person, as it may be seen as rejection. Creating psychological distance might be wiser. Aldo Civico is an experienced negotiator in the conflict zones of Sardinia and Colombia. In a talk to the Association of Northern Mediators, he described a technique he uses to protect himself from feeling fear. He says he imagines a translucent screen protecting him from object of fear; he can still hear and see the person, but the fear does not get through.

Positivity

Since a seminal study on optimism and health in 1985 (Scheier and Carver 1985), researchers have been finding evidence that positive people are more successful, live longer, and have more fulfilled lives. So, how can we be positive when something bad happens?

Try using the tool below on a negative situation. It is best to start with a minor annoyance and use it frequently. Eventually, it will even help with major disasters.

Sad to Glad Tool

An exercise to change your perspective on mishaps and mistakes

G: What **good** can you see? What can you be **grateful** for? **Guess** what benefit it might bring.

L: What can you **learn** from this situation? What can you **laugh** about? Is there anything **lucky**?

A: What **action** would make the situation better? **Acknowledge** your part. **Ask** what now? **Ask for help** if needed.

D: **Decide** not to let this ruin your day. **Distract** yourself. **Distance** yourself.

This works for most things, but start with something small first.

Worked example

For example, I have dropped a bottle of milk, spilling it over the floor.

G: It is good I have plenty of milk. Grateful it did not go on my clothes; I guess someone might help me clean it up and save me having to wash the floor this evening.

L: I have learned that I should watch where I put the milk and not to try and do 2 things at once. I am laughing at myself treating spilled milk as an exercise. It is lucky I have plenty of time this morning.

A: Instead of feeling bad, I can clean up. Or, I could ask someone to help. I am aware it was my fault.

D: Well, it will not ruin my day. I will just forget about it now and get on with having a great day.

Note the good things as much as—if not more than—the bad things, and look for the good in everything.

Eventually, we will find (mostly in retrospect, of course) that we can be very grateful to those people who have made life most difficult for us.

Ayya Knema

Having a more positive outlook will not only make you less likely to get caught in the whirlpool of conflict, but it will also help you recover more quickly.

Practice

We are what we repeatedly do. Excellence, then, is not an act, but a habit.

Aristotle

Professionals working in high-stress situations learn to work effectively by practicing in simulations, minor incidents, and drills. The same strategy can be used for controlling emotions, fear, and anger, and keeping our thinking brains switched on.

Use small negative events to practice positivity and control. Practice what you might say or do in incidents. Take part in role plays and simulations. See annoyances as opportunities to practice your self-control. Disagreements become chances to test your skills. When you see something as an opportunity to learn, you will be less threatened and more motivated.

Persist

If you can't fly, then run, if you can't run then walk. If you can't walk then crawl, but whatever you do, you have to keep moving forward.

Martin Luther King, Jr.

Learning effectiveness and poise in stressful situations takes time, effort, and most of all, patience (a bonus "pea"). Keep looking and learning from what worked and what did not.

If we look at each instance of conflict or challenge and analyze the effect of our actions and resolve to try afresh the next time, we will keep moving forward and improving.

Accept that conflict is inevitable, and that you cannot prevent it. What you can do with every instance is learn. Understand your emotions and work out what to do better next time. At worst, we can use a difficult situation as a lesson. At best, we can manage conflict so well that relationships are strengthened and objectives achieved.

Check Understanding Chapter 3

- What are the six "peas" for staying calm?
- Which one is the most important?
- Which of these strategies are you already using?
- Which exercise did you find most helpful?
- What drawbacks are there to the posture suggestions?
- Try out one of the strategies you have not used the next time you feel stressed.

CHAPTER 4

Speak up or Stay Silent?

Figuring out whether it is worth bringing up a controversial issue

One of the biggest barriers to resolving conflict and interpersonal relations is the fear of vulnerability. Another is lack of skills. People do not know how to manage difficult topics, sensitive situations, or touchy people. How often do we hear the following sentiments?

> I know it's wrong, but if I bring it up, people might think I'm self-righteous.
> I don't want to cause a fuss.
> Speak out? It's more than my job's worth.
> Say something? Last time I tried that, I got shouted at.
> It's nothing to do with me, why should I risk saying anything?
> Speak out? Why bother—it won't make any difference.
> I don't want to be mean.

Health and safety is an excellent example. Although failing to speak out when you see someone doing something dangerous carries penalties, people still do not say anything because they do not want to look boring or were shouted at when they spoke up before. There is also the danger that speaking out and distracting someone at the wrong moment can cause the very accident you wanted to prevent.

On the one hand, speaking out might create even more problems. On the other, not speaking out also has consequences. How can we work out what is the best option? This chapter is primarily about when you are involved in conflict. Chapter 9 offers more guidance on whether to speak up when others are in conflict and you are not directly involved.

Ask Yourself

Sometimes, it is very clear—a broken promise, an important issue, or a clearly dangerous practice. Other times, we really do not know, so we tend to keep quiet as that seems the safest bet (in the short term, at least). Based on their research in work situations, the *Crucial Confrontations* team (Patterson, Grenny and McMillan, et al. 2005) recommend you ask yourself the following questions before deciding when to speak out and when to stay silent.

- Am I acting out my concerns instead of speaking?
- Is my conscience nagging me?
- Am I assessing the situation accurately?
- Will it make a difference?

What is behind these questions? Let us look a bit deeper.

Behavior

Because people want to avoid conflict, they will do almost anything rather than engage in conversation about the controversial issues. Icy politeness is a common way of dealing with conflict. Another is gossiping to others about the person's failings instead of talking to the individual concerned. You may find yourself reluctant to help or work with certain people. Are you making sarcastic comments? Are you taking out your frustration on others? Do you find yourself acting unkindly, and then, justifying it? Are you acting out your feelings instead of talking about them?

If the situation impacting your life is changing your behavior significantly, this is a sign that you need to act to resolve the situation.

Instinct

Is the situation keeping you awake at night? Are you torn between what you want to do and what you know is right? Or, do you feel uncomfortable with what you are being asked to do? Are you keeping yourself too busy to think about the situation? You may feel ill at the thought of the situation. Defensiveness is often a sign that you are feeling unsure of the rectitude of your position. Pause and listen to your inner voice.

If your conscience is nagging you, you need to resolve the inner conflict, speak out, or leave the situation.

Ignoring Risks of Silence

We often excuse our silence by saying, "Well, if it was that important, someone else would say something." Keeping quiet about health and safety issues can cost lives. Even minor conflicts, if suppressed, can rankle and sour a working atmosphere. Hand in hand with downplaying the risks of keeping quiet is the exaggeration of the dangers of speaking up. We imagine that that our jobs are on the line or that speaking up will destroy relationships.

Sit down and work out the worst consequences of keeping silent and the worst-case scenario if you speak up. Then, list the best consequences of staying quiet and of speaking out. Now, being practical and logical, look at what is most likely to happen, and how you could handle it if it did happen.

Significance

We often excuse ourselves by saying, "It won't make a difference anyways." Is this true in your situation? How do you know? Would it make a difference to how you feel? Would others be encouraged to speak up if you did? A related question is "How could you speak up and be heard?"

The video, *One Simple Skill to Overcome Peer Pressure* (Grenny and Maxfield 2015), vividly illustrates the power of even one dissenting voice. They reenacted Solomon Asch's experiment in conformity (Asch 1951) by showing teenagers two cards. One card had three lines of distinctly different lengths, labelled A, B, and C. The reference card had a line which was obviously the same length as line C. The teenagers were asked to speak out in turn and say which line was the same length as the reference card. The first five people were plants and answered A, which was obviously wrong. Yet, 95 percent of the others, despite showing visible signs of doubt, answered A. They then repeated the experiment with one of the five politely stating that his view was different and he thought it was C. In this case, all the rest of the teenagers found the courage to state the correct answer.

You may think this is because teenagers are particularly susceptible to peer pressure. However, Grenny and Maxfield found that other groups were also affected, with all groups showing at least two-thirds of people giving the wrong answer when the initial answers were all wrong.

One person speaking up can make a difference. A skilful intervention can tip the balance.

When to Stay Silent

There are times when it is better to walk away or to keep silent. There is no hard or fast rule, it depends on the situation and our values. Here is a list of factors to consider, and we will cover these in detail below.

- Safety
- Information
- Motive
- Time and Place
- Importance
- Consequences

Safety

Sometimes, it is not safe to speak out—for example, if someone is holding a weapon or is too angry to listen to reason. You may be in a vulnerable situation with your job, or speaking out may place someone in danger. Safety may not override other concerns, but it should be considered.

Information

Do you have all the information? Is there part of the picture you cannot see? We often leap to conclusions and condemn others' behavior without considering their intentions or reasons. Before speaking up, be sure you have the right information.

Motive

What is your motive for speaking up? Is it to help someone improve or is it an attempt to humiliate them? Be honest with yourself about your motive. Sometimes, we speak out as a weapon, especially if we feel angry or hurt. Would you feel proud or ashamed if you spoke out?

Time and Place

Is this the right time and place to speak out? Choosing an appropriate time and place increases the odds of success. For example, criticizing someone in public may lead to a confrontation or shutdown, rather than discussion or learning. In another case, a public statement may be needed to make a difference. Waiting too long to speak out may send the wrong message, yet speaking quickly before you have enough information may cause more damage.

There are no hard and fast rules. Taking time and place into consideration will help you manage conflict more successfully.

Importance

How important is this issue? Choosing your battles is a wise strategy. It takes energy and effort to speak up well, and may upset people. Is the issue one that really matters, or is it a minor annoyance? Go over the consequences of staying silent—will it matter? Sometimes, what seems to be a minor issue may be a sign of a deeper problem. For example, never asking a colleague if they would like a cup of tea might be simple selfishness or thoughtlessness. Or, it may be a calculated attempt to make the person feel an outsider.

Consequences

Will speaking out cause more harm than not speaking out? What are the real dangers? Go back to the questions you asked yourself. What is the likelihood that the situation will improve without intervention? What benefits would there be if speaking up resolved the issue? What would happen if you did not speak up?

Although it seems a long process to go through, in reality, it only takes a few minutes. The more you practice assessing these factors, the more natural and swift the process becomes.

Desire to Protect Others

Sometimes, we keep quiet because we do not want to hurt others' feelings. This is common in managers of charities or caring professions, such as nursing or teaching. They think of themselves as nice people who care about others, so they shrink from criticism and addressing problems. Gentle hints are dropped, and the issue is left until it either goes away or explodes.

Understanding that we are not responsible for the feelings and actions of others is key to moving forward in this situation.

A primary reason many of us stay in silence rather than connecting honestly is that we misunderstand our responsibility for others' emotions. We are responsible to care about how others feel, but we are not responsible for how they feel. Their emotions are their choices. How we act can affect them—and we should always act with compassion and respect. But that is where our duty stops. When you take responsibility for others' feelings, you begin to live dishonestly. You begin to calculate and manipulate in order to control others' feelings. And by so doing, you surrender the possibility of both solving problems and connecting deeply.

Joseph Grenny

By neglecting to talk to the person about the problem, you are denying them the knowledge and chance of putting things right. I trained customer service staff to say Thank You to the people complaining. Why? Because a complaint told us that they were not happy and gave us the chance to change things. If customers had walked away instead of communicating their displeasure, we would have continued upsetting people and lost business.

SCIM Tool: Deciding to Speak Up or Not

This helps you remember the key factors to consider when you are wondering whether to speak up.

S: Is it **safe**? Is it **sensible** to speak up now or will it be wise to wait?

C: What are the **consequences** if I do not speak up? What does my **conscience** say? What do I need to **consider**?

I: What is **important**? Do I have all the **information** I need?

M: What is my **motive** in speaking out? What skills do I need to make my **meaning** clear? Is this the best **method** to improve the situation?

The SCIM Tool is designed to help you quickly skim through the questions you need to ask before you decide whether to speak up or not.

The Risk Assessment Tool in Chapter 12 may also be helpful in working out whether to speak up. Chapters 9 and 10 give more details on risks and responsibilities.

Once you have worked through the questions and you have decided you need to speak out, what then? The next chapter will help you prepare for having that difficult conversation.

Check Understanding Chapter 4

- How important is environment and culture in whether we speak up?
- Do you tend to stay silent or speak up?
- What are your main reasons for staying silent?
- List some of the things you should think about when deciding whether to speak up or stay silent.
- What risks are there if you stay silent?
- Think of an example of a conflict you have been in (or are likely to be involved in) and use the SCIM tool to work out if you should speak up or stay silent.

CHAPTER 5

Getting Ready to Take the Plunge

Managing your thoughts and preparing

The common view of a mediator and conflict management coach is someone who stops people arguing or teaches them to control their temper. I do that; however, I spend just as much time starting awkward conversations and helping people speak up effectively.

Starting a difficult conversation is a bit like getting ready for a bath. Imagine you had a really busy, tense day, your muscles are aching and you are exhausted. You know a nice long soak in the bath would make you feel better. But you would have to trail upstairs, run the bath, undress, and you just cannot be bothered.

And you might have to clean out the bath and maybe there isn't any hot water and it takes too long and maybe it will not work.

So, you ignore your aching muscles and stress. . .and it gets worse. (Or you may hit the wine, which helps for a bit, but then, you end up with a hangover).

How is starting an awkward conversation like deciding to take a bath?

In both cases, we know what we need to do to ease the pain and that once it is sorted, we will benefit. . .but it is the hassle in between and the chance that things go wrong that puts us off starting.

We ignore or mutter about our problems until they do get better, we explode or get ill. We all put up with discomfort and a real chance of things getting worse because we fear change or are stuck in our present pain.

Unlike running a bath, few of us are taught how to start an awkward conversation and make it turn out well. However, it is a skill and you can learn it. People who can do this are far more successful in life, love, and work than those who do not. We will never be perfect—we are human; however, this skill will make life easier and pleasanter.

Motivating Yourself to Act

Looking at what motivated me to get up and take that bath illustrates some useful steps in motivating you to take the plunge and have that necessary but difficult conversation.

Acknowledge Present Pain

I recognized that I was aching and stressed.

Ask yourself, "What pain am I putting up with?" Do not deny or ignore the situation. What is it costing you to stay where you are?

Focus on Positive Result

I thought of a nice warm bath, the tension seeping away, the aches and pains vanishing.

Ask yourself, "What would it be like if this conversation went well? How would it feel?" Allow yourself to visualize a future without this stress or conflict.

Realistic Assessment

Was having to clean the bath before I started such a big problem compared to my pain? How high was the chance of no hot water?

Ask yourself, "What is it worth to get rid of my present pain?" We tend to overestimate the risks and underestimate the chances of success. Try and be more objective. What is the worst that can happen? How would you deal with it?

Alternatives

There were alternatives to the bath, but they either were not as appealing or unrealistic.

Ask yourself, "What are my options here?" In mediation, we encourage people to think of both the best and worst-case scenarios. This helps place the situation into perspective.

Next Steps

Engaging in mental exercises such as the ones mentioned earlier have an added bonus of calming your primitive brain and engaging your logic. Once you have weighed up what you want and where you are, you are calm enough to plan, to perform well and succeed.

Having worked out the pain I was in and the benefits of having a bath, I was more realistic about the risks–there would be hot water, but I would almost certainly have to scrub the bath before I ran it. That minor hassle compared to the major benefit made the decision easy. You may find that the pain is not that great, or there is another solution.

Getting Ready

Just as I had to find the towels, scrub the bath, undress, and run the bath, so you need to prepare for the awkward conversation or potential confrontation.

Clarity and Calm

Be clear about what you need. Being clear about what is important and what you need before you start is crucial. Have you got all the facts? Is there any other interpretation of the situation?

Try and see the situation from others' viewpoints. Make sure you have control of your emotions and your stories. Do not go into a potential confrontation angry or frightened. (If you are feeling nervous or flustered, try the one of the tools in Chapter 3).

Accept Responsibility

Just as I should have kept the bath clean, maybe there is something that you did that contributed to the situation. Can you change anything or do something to make it easier to have this conversation? Do you need to put something right? Apologize? (See Chapter 12 for resources and Chapter 10 for how to put things right.)

Do what you can to make it work before taking the plunge. What did you do to contribute to the problem?

Test the Water

No one sensible leaps into a bath without checking the temperature of the water.

So, ask permission before you start. Here is a suggestion—but use your own words. "I really value our relationship. There's something that's bothering me and I'd like your help in sorting it out. When would be a good time?"

Sometimes, we think the bath is fine, then realize it is actually too hot—and either need to add cold water or get out. So, too, in difficult conversations, we sometimes need to act to make sure that everyone feels safe and calm enough to talk about the situation in a way that resolves things.

Consideration

Show consideration for the feelings of others. Choose a time and place that lends itself to a meaningful conversation. Start by showing your respect and concern for the other person. Go into the meeting with an intention to show kindness and to listen. Look for things you have in common and that you like about the person. Think about how this conversation could benefit both of you.

Hope

Keep your ideal outcome in mind, and go in determined to do all you can to bring it about. Professor Richard Wiseman (Wiseman 2003) found that those who expect good things to happen are more fortunate than those who do not. Our expectations color our behavior, show through our body language, and affect our mood. If you fear things will go badly, you are more likely to trigger the flight/fight/freeze response and turn off the thinking bit of your brain, just when you need it most.

CATCH sums up what you need to remember before going into a potential awkward situation or confrontation.

CATCH Tool

CATCH yourself before you start a difficult conversation . . .

    C. Clarify in your own mind what the problem is. When did it start, what exactly is happening, what are the results? Try and see it from all angles.

    A. Accept responsibility for what you might have done—did you explain yourself clearly?

    T. Test the water. Ask permission. Take it slow.

    C. Consideration. Be curious, not furious. If you are angry, you will not think straight. Remember the good in the others; try and see their point of view.

    H. Hope for a good outcome—think of the best possible result from your discussion. How can you make sure that happens?

Now you have prepared yourself, Chapter 6 guides you through the awkward conversation and highlights some key points.

Check Understanding Chapter 5

- Do you find it hard to start conversations about delicate situations?
- How could you motivate yourself to speak up when you feel it is right?
- What fears or obstacles hold you back?
- What do you need to do before acting?
- Why is having hope in a good outcome important?
- Think of an example of a conflict you are likely to be involved in and use the CATCH tool to prepare yourself.

CHAPTER 6

Difficult Conversations

How to manage a conversation where there is tension

In this chapter, I give some key principles on easing tension and then go into more depth. This chapter deals with situations where all parties want to resolve the conflict and are committed to try and do so. Chapter 8 will look at more complex cases, such as where one party does not want to engage in discussion or where you are in a position where you cannot or do not want to discuss things with the other person. For example, one partner in a bitter divorce may not want to engage, but the other needs to find a way of dealing with her anger and moving forwards. Or where the other party is your employer and you really need your job. There may be a lack of trust and concerns about safety. Knowing the general principles covered in this chapter will be helpful in all situations, and form a basis on which to build a strategy for more complex situations.

Key Points

I have given some examples of dialogue, but it is much better if you can put things into your own words. Practice these principles as often as you can in everyday conversations, watching for reactions and learning what works for you. Knowing your strengths and what you are good at helps you work out the best strategy for you. Understanding the strengths and good points of the others involved, as well as their problems, will help you see the situation from a wider perspective.

Before you start, pause, "catch yourself" (see Chapter 5) and make sure you have the right frame of mind.

The key points during the conversation are:

- Ask permission
- Show respect and consideration
- Explain the problem without blame
- Ask for their point of view
- Listen
- Tell your story
- Ask for their feedback/solution
- Explore areas of agreement
- Agree next steps

Ask Permission

If the other person hasn't raised the topic, ask permission to talk about it. Be clear about time scales and the importance of the issue.

"There's something that's really been bothering me and I wonder if I could speak with you about it before the weekend."

Be clear about why you want to talk about it and what's in it for them.

"There are some issues we need to resolve before we present the project at the launch next Friday."

If they say no, ask when would be a good time and place. If they don't want to talk, your options will vary depending on the situation (see Chapter 8).

Show Respect/Concern

When you ask for "a word" or say something is bothering you, the message the other person receives is "problem ahead." This starts to trigger the Flight/Fight/Freeze Response. To keep them open and receptive, you need to show respect and concern for the person. To calm them and keep their logical brains switched on, show respect and concern. Be careful not to pretend. People can see through false courtesy very swiftly and it will make the situation worse. Asking permission is one way of showing respect. If you don't like the person, think of how you would like to be spoken to or how you would speak to someone you care about. Act as if this is the case. Talk about the things you agree on or that the person has achieved.

"I really appreciate you working overtime on the project last week, and it's great we have managed to complete the first section. I value your attention to detail and your contribution to the team."

Explain the Problem Without Blame

Be objective and talk about your part in the process. Talk tentatively, briefly outline your observations and feelings and ask for feedback. This requires courage as we are all reluctant to show our vulnerability and admit our part in the problem.

Avoiding blame and admitting your contribution to the problem goes against the grain. However, if you don't, the other person will undoubtedly bring it up as in the example below. If you do admit your failings, most people will react generously.

Practical Example

It's Not Me, It's You

Manager: When you interrupted me in the middle of the presentation at the last meeting, you made me look stupid. Everyone thought it was very rude and you made people think the team were disorganised. I was furious.

IT Person: Well, you got it wrong! It was obviously wrong, and I don't want the team to be blamed for that. I had to say something. You shouldn't be so touchy about things. It would have been worse if I hadn't spoken up. I can't believe you're complaining about this.

Try this instead

(Continued)

Manager: "I know I got a detail wrong at the presentation today. When you corrected me in public in the middle of my presentation, I felt humiliated. I also think it makes the team look bad when mistakes occur. What's your view on what happened?"

IT Person: I was embarrassed for the team, because it was obviously wrong, and it made us look like we were idiots. I felt I had to speak up to make sure they realised that you just mis-spoke. I wasn't trying to make you look bad, I was trying to save the situation.

Ask the Other's View

"Seek First to Understand," one of Covey's *Seven Habits of Highly Effective People* (S. R. Covey 2004), is key to managing conflict. The natural tendency is to rush in and give our side of the story.

There is no greater agony than bearing an untold story inside you

Maya Angelou

Yet, if we listen to the other side first, we are more likely to achieve our objectives. There are four reasons for this.

1. We get more information about the situation which may help us see things differently or understand the issues better.
2. It shows respect and consideration.
3. Having the chance to speak allows the other person to name their feelings and calm down. We also have a chance to reflect on our story and its accuracy
4. Feeling heard makes people more likely to listen to others.

However, the benefits of asking the other side to speak first are lost if we don't listen attentively and fully. If we make one of the mistakes below, the other person will recognise we are not listening, and will feel hurt and angry.

1. Our mind starts to wander and we start thinking of something else
2. We start working out what to say next
3. We judge and comment internally on what the other person is saying
4. We listen to find ways of proving ourselves right or discover weaknesses in their case.

You may think that others might not notice this happening. However, our body language and facial expressions give us away. People may not know **why** they feel you are not listening, but they **will** notice. So, learning to listen is a key aspect of managing difficult conversations well.

Listen

Attentive listening is a crucial skill, not just in conflict management, but in persuading and influencing people in every sphere of life. This is the heart of conflict resolution, and the one essential skill you need to master. Spend as much time as possible learning to be a good listener and you will benefit enormously. Chapter 7 covers this and other conversational skills in greater depth. A study at the National University of Singapore (Swee and Schimer 2015) has shown that saying OW can reduce physical pain. Other research (Bruneau and Saxe 2012) shows that once a person feels heard and understood, they feel better, even if nothing has changed.

> The most important thing is that we need to be understood. We need someone to be able to listen to us and to understand us. Then we will suffer less.
>
> Thich Nhat Hanh

Listening is not judging or waiting your turn. It is trying to understand the other person's view and hear their story. Try and see the feeling and needs behind their words, and be aware of body language, tone and expressions.

Tell Your Story

Now that you have the chance to tell your side, pause for a moment. Thank the other person for helping you understand their side. Remind yourself of your ideal outcome and consider how best to achieve this when expressing yourself.

First, explain objectively what you have observed, without criticism or judgement. Don't make assumptions about the other person's intentions or thoughts. Acknowledge where there might be a different interpretation or where information is missing. Don't gloss over your failings, take responsibility and admit if you've got it wrong. It is best to try and handle one problem at a time. Giving a whole catalogue of complaints will be counterproductive.

Talk tentatively. "I'd like to explain how I see the situation." Start by describing the situation or series of events as objectively and clearly as you can. Avoid making assumptions or assigning motives. Be as clear as possible without blaming or criticizing.

If this is the first time you have had a chance to tell your story, it is helpful to write it out, rehearse with a good listener or practice out loud before the conversation with the other person. This will allow you to vent emotions and rephrase things that may be misunderstood.

Take responsibility for anything you may have done to contribute to the problem, without defensiveness. This is very difficult and there may be occasions where doing this may put you at risk. Yet if you have erred and don't admit it, it will create barriers and mistrust. This requires courage as we are all reluctant to show our vulnerability and admit our part in the problem. Don't become defensive or justify your actions. When we say, "It wasn't my fault" the other person hears "It was your fault" or "You should understand." If you want understanding and forgiveness, don't ruin an apology with an excuse. The sections called "I'm Wrong" in Chapter 8 and "Apologising" in Chapter 10 give more detail on this topic.

Once you have set out what happened objectively, let them know your feelings *without blaming* them for your emotions. Don't say "you made me feel" but simply, "I felt." Use descriptive but not emotional words that could be blaming. For example: if you say, "I felt betrayed," that implies that the other person betrayed you. If you say, "I felt very sad and alone," that simply describes how you feel.

For example, "I felt alone and miserable when everyone went off together for drinks after work." instead of "You made me feel isolated and shunned when no one asked me to go for drinks after work." It might be that everyone thought you would just come along. Or maybe they thought someone had asked you.

Describe what you need as a request, rather than a demand

State what you need and request what you would like them to do. "I'd like to feel part of the team. Would you all like to come out together for drinks one night so that I could get to know you better?"

Be careful not to demand, but be clear about what you need. Watch for signs of misunderstanding or anger and address them. Speak in a way that makes it easy to listen, showing respect and understanding. Keep to the point. Check understanding.

> We can say what we need to say. We can gently, but assertively, speak our mind. We do not need to be judgmental, tactless, blaming or cruel when we speak our truths.
>
> Melody Beattie

Ask for Their Solution

We often rush in with our solutions because we want to resolve the issue and move on. This can limit our options, as well as generating resistance. Asking the other party for their solution brings up other options and ways of looking at the problem. They may suggest what you were going to propose—or their idea might be better. Suggest that before looking at whether options are feasible, you both (or all the parties) make a written list of several ways to partially or fully resolving the situation. Don't judge or criticise each other's ideas, but simply write them down. Getting together to find a solution to the problem not only brings you together in a common cause but also generates more creative ideas.

Seek Common Ground

List what the ideas you agree on and which options have potential. Discover common goals or values. Do this before finding fault with the solutions. Look with an attitude of "what might be acceptable" or "what changes would we need to make for you to feel comfortable with this idea?"

Work out priorities. It may be that something is not that important to you, but is critical for the other person. Try and figure out a solution that meets the most important needs of both parties first. If this looks difficult, find small things you can agree on, and if there is a way that both of you could have at least some of your needs met. You may need a break and to start again another day. Be patient and positive.

Commit and Follow up

Once you have agreed things, it is helpful to write down what each party has agreed to do. In some cultures, this is expected. In others, people may see a written document as evidence of mistrust. Be sure that everyone understands that any document is simply to clarify who will do what and when. Make sure that everyone is clear about what is expected and the timescale is clear. Even if you don't agree on everything, try and find something that can be done to move forward or resolve the issue. It may be a date for another meeting, an agreement to call in a professional or look at alternative methods of resolving the dispute.

End the meeting with appreciation, even if it isn't an ideal outcome, you should have more clarity.

Sample Resolutions

Now look at the example from Chapter 1, repeated below.

Think about where things started to go wrong. See if you can identify what could have been done differently. What unseen factors might have added to the problem?

Practical Example: Painting Problem

Sylvia had asked Rosie's firm to paint all the corridors in the office block over the weekend so that the work could be done when the offices were empty. When Sylvia came in on Monday morning, one corridor had not been done. All the painting gear had been left in the corridor. She was very upset as some important clients were visiting that day and

(Continued)

would be using that corridor. Sylvia didn't wait until she got in to her office, but rang Rosie straightaway to ask what was happening. Rosie wasn't in, so Sylvia left an angry message on her answer phone. Sylvia was so upset and stressed that she snapped at her PA. The PA was hurt as she was just going to suggest a solution, but as Sylvia was horrible to her, she didn't bother. Sylvia blamed Rosie for making her annoyed.

Meanwhile, Rosie had picked up the angry message. Rosie was furious as the reason they had not finished the corridor was because Sylvia had said that she had enough paint to do all the job, and but this was not the case. Rosie had tried to contact Sylvia without success over the weekend and had left a note on her desk to say the painters would be in once they had bought more paint. Rosie didn't stop to think that Sylvia might not have seen her note. She dashed off an angry email and was so upset that she had to go for a walk to calm down before getting down to work. She decided not to bother going to Sylvia's office because of her attitude. When Sylvia got Rosie's email, she was livid.

Soon there was a flood of angry emails and texts flying back and forth. Both became stressed and angry and this spilled over into their work and private lives.

Sylvia spent the first few minutes with the important clients complaining about the terrible painters. The clients thought she was unprofessional and not focussed on their needs, so decide not to use her firm. Sylvia blamed Rosie for this and decided to consult a lawyer to see if she could sue. Her PA went home and complained to her mother about her terrible boss and started looking for a new job.

Rosie was so upset that she went home and complained to her husband all evening. He got so fed up that he asked her why she carried on with customers like that—and she decided that she would not do any more work for Sylvia. Rosie felt so upset about everything that her ulcer started playing up. She couldn't focus on the estimates she needed to that evening so lost a job by not getting the estimate in on time.

Neither was aware of the work that wasn't getting done, the reason for their headaches or how easily the problem could have been sorted.

This potentially could end up in court, with Sylvia refusing to pay Rosie's bill or with Rosie claiming Sylvia was unreasonable. They would both suffer even more with more time and money invested in litigation. Certainly, the relationship between them was damaged. Rosie might have lost other customers when Sylvia told people about how she hadn't finished the work (without telling them why). Rosie could also damage Sylvia's reputation about complaining about her behaviour.

As with any conflict, there is no one right answer. Rather than look for fault or judging, think of as many possible solutions as you can. Here are two scenarios where the conflict doesn't escalate, because one of the parties managed things better.

Painting Problem Solved by Sylvia

When Sylvia came in on Monday morning, and saw that the corridor had not been painted, and all the equipment lying there, she was very upset. She tried ringing Rosie, but she wasn't in, so Sylvia just said, "Please call me urgently. Thank you." Sylvia realised that she couldn't do any more about it now, so went through to her office. She told her PA about the situation, who said she had seen the note from Rosie about the problem. They discussed an alternative plan for the important visit. Sylvia was glad she hadn't left an angry message. Rosie had said how much paint she needed and Sylvia had got it wrong. When Rosie got in from buying the paint, she rang Sylvia. Sylvia apologised about the shortage of paint and explained about the important visit. Rosie offered to come in straight away and finish the corridor or move the painting gear before the visitors came, whichever fitted best with Sylvia.

Painting Problem Resolved by Rosie

Rosie got back from buying the paint and heard the angry message from Sylvia on her office answerphone, complaining about the mess of all the equipment and how that this would impact on her business because the visiting customers would think she was messy and

(Continued)

disorganised. "Oh dear" Rosie thought, "Sylvia obviously hasn't seen my note of explanation. I'll need to help sort this out." Rather than try and justify her actions (which Sylvia would have felt was blaming her), Rosie sent a brief text to say "Enroute with more paint. Will sort things out ASAP." By this time, Sylvia has seen the note and was feeling a bit ashamed of her outburst. When Rosie came, she didn't blame Sylvia, she just said, "I'm sorry this happened today. What would be best for you—if I took away the gear and came back later, or quickly painted the corridor?" By allowing Sylvia to save face, Rosie earned herself a loyal customer and great advocate for her business.

Of course, not everyone will behave reasonably even if you do. There is more chance of resolving conflict in a productive way if you can control your emotions and engage with the other person. If you find you are rushing and reacting, review Chapter 2 and Chapter 3. If you are reluctant to start the conversation or don't know whether to engage, read Chapter 4. If you need help with specific skills see Chapter 7.

Figure 6.1 gives some hints on what NOT to do, what to DO and what to TRY.

In situations of low trust or chronic misunderstanding, one conversation will not solve years of problems. But it may be enough to

Don't	Do	Try
Hurry	Take time	Sit down
Assume	Ask what they need	Summarise
Say you know how they feel	Empathise	Clarify
Talk too much	Listen carefully	Asking what they need
Gloss over your part	Acknowledge distress	Offer what you can
Blame	Start a dialogue	Apologise for the situation
Ignore non-verbal signals	Be aware of your own body language as well as that of others	Matching your tone and speed to the other— without parroting or aping

Figure 6.1 Tips on Having a Difficult Conversation

slow or reverse the escalation of conflict. Talking is a start, but behaviour needs to be consistent with what was promised or shown.

You can't talk your way out of problems you behave yourself into.

Stephen Covey

Check Understanding Chapter 6

- Which stage of an awkward conversation do you find most challenging?
- Why is it important to avoid blame?
- What reasons are there for asking the other person to speak first?
- List some things you could do that would make it more likely that people will listen to you.
- Think of some instances where you did some of the things in the "Don't" column of Figure 6.1. What happened? What could you have done instead?

CHAPTER 7

Improving Communication

Key Skills and Considerations to Improve your Communication

Good communication is key to resolving most conflicts, and poor communication is often the cause of conflict. Many people think communicating is broadcasting information. There are endless courses on presentation and public speaking skills. Social media advisors encourage us to send out information frequently.

Communication is not just about how you speak or write, it is just as much about how you listen and receive. There is noise and information flowing into our lives from many different sources. Everyone wants to speak and no one wants to listen. With so many inputs, our brains tune things out, our attention flits off to the next thing. Learning to listen well is a powerful tool not just for understanding, but for influencing as well.

Listening: Ting

Chinese characters are pictograms, and are composed of characters (or parts of them) representing other words. Ting, the Chinese character for listening (Figure 7.1), can be broken down in various ways, although all are similar. It symbolizes the key components of a good listener. It is a useful visual reminder, just like the Six Peas.

Ears

Of course, you need ears to listen. Remember the old saying that you have two ears and one mouth, so you should listen twice as much as speak. If you

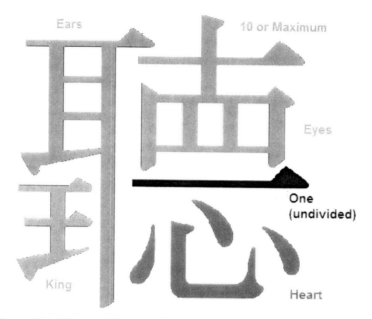

Figure 7.1 Chinese Character for Listening

cannot hear the person clearly, adjust your position or ask them to speak more slowly or more loudly. One client was reluctant to tell people he was deaf. Because people did not know he had not heard, they were annoyed when he did not follow instructions. Because listening was hard when he could not hear clearly, he often mentally switched off during meetings. This switching off was obvious and resulted in considerable problems and irritation. People thought he was rude or unmotivated. Once they realized that he had a problem hearing, they saw his behavior in a different light.

Listen to the tone of the voice, the words they use, what they do not say, and the silences.

People start to heal the moment they feel heard.

Cheryl Richardson

Listening, though is not **just** hearing, but making meaning from sound.

King (or Mind)

This has a double meaning. One is that the person should be treated respectfully, like a king. Medieval nobles listened to the words and intonations of their sovereigns extremely carefully, as a misunderstanding could be fatal. While we are unlikely to be in such a situation, not paying attention will damage the success of the interaction. Think as a medieval noble—what does the king need? How does he feel?

The second is that the mind should be in control, not our feelings. We must manage our emotions and not allow them to get in the way of understanding the other person. Calm yourself so that your logical brain is in control.

> One of the most sincere forms of respect is actually listening to what another has to say.
>
> Bryant H. McGill

Maximum

The Chinese figure ten symbolizes maximum, and as a part of the word "attention," reminds us how we should listen. How do you show that another's message is of maximum importance? Silence, accompanied by nods or nonverbal sounds such as *mmhmm* is one sign. Another might be leaning toward someone or meeting their eyes. Body language varies from culture to culture, so take care that your behavior is not misinterpreted. Wait until the person has finished speaking. Ask relevant questions or paraphrase.

> Listening doesn't happen by itself. It takes a conscious decision and a willingness to release the distraction of being right. In learning how to listen, we develop the virtues of patience and even humility. Ultimately, listening teaches us to resolve conflict by letting it resolve itself.
>
> Brian Muldoon

Eyes

Does it seem odd to talk about eyes and listening? Think about the last time you were talking to someone. Did they look at you or keep an eye on the television? Eyes are expressive as well—what are your eyes saying while you are listening? Remember that appropriate eye contact differs in many cultures. If someone does not meet your eye, it may be cultural, rather than an indication of lying. But if your eyes flick to your watch or your phone, it sends a message that you are not listening, whatever culture you are from.

Use your eyes to gather nonverbal signals from their body language. Is someone tense or angry? Does their expression match their words?

> Because you're always communicating, even when you're not talking - with your body language, your facial expressions, your eyes.
>
> Orlando Bloom

Undivided

Receiving someone's undivided attention is a great and rare gift. We cannot listen if we are trying to do something else at the same time. Multitasking may seem like a great way of saving time. Recent research proves that not only does multitasking slow down your processing (Gorlick 2014), it reduces your IQ, and permanently damages your brain. But in this context, multitasking shows disrespect and alienates the other person. So, turn the phone off, hang a Do Not Disturb sign on the door, and focus your undivided attention on the other person.

> You cannot truly listen to anyone and do anything else at the same time.
>
> Scott Peck

Heart

If you do not want to listen or have already made up your mind, it will show, no matter how good an actor you may be. Open your heart and mind to the other person. If you behave kindly toward someone, you start to feel more compassionate toward them. This openness and kindness works wonders.

> The smallest act of kindness is worth more than the greatest intention.
>
> Kahlil Gibran

But how do we handle feelings of aversion? At a talk for the Association of Northern Mediators in York in 2014, Dr John Sturrock, an internationally renowned mediator, was asked how a mediator should react to an evil person. Dr Sturrock said that his response was to wonder what would drive someone to do something like that. Being curious about the causes of someone's behavior is more productive than being furious about the end result. So, when you come to listen, put your views to one side and try and understand why the other party might feel the way they do. There is no need to agree, disagree, or evaluate at the start. Just listen. Separate the person from the behavior. Open your heart.

Nonverbal Communication

Dr Sandy Pentland of the MIT Human Dynamics Lab devised an array of technology called a sociometer to study nonverbal behavior in social interactions. Through motion sensors, microphones, and infrared transmitters/receivers, the researchers could track physical movements, vocal inflections, and proximity. After analyzing the data from hundreds of interactions in different settings, they discovered that there were patterns which showed the degree of engagement. By looking for the patterns without assessing the verbal content of the conversations, Pentland's group could predict with over 70 percent accuracy whether the participants would want to continue the contact (for example, whether they would exchange cards or numbers). Nonverbal communication is extremely important in building trust (Hardesty 2010).

Be aware of cultural differences in nonverbal communication. In India, shaking the head by turning from side to side means no, as it does in many other countries. However, tilting the head to the right shoulder, then the left shoulder means okay. In some countries, frequent eye contact is positive and shows signs of interest. In other countries, avoiding eye contact is a sign of respect. Arabic cultures believe prolonged eye contact helps them understand the truthfulness of the other person. Someone from another culture may see this prolonged eye contact as a sign of sexual interest and feel uncomfortable. Touching and where we touch varies from culture to culture. We need to be aware that even something as simple as pointing may be misconstrued.

However, one can mitigate potential mistrust by watching for signs of discomfort from others and asking how they feel. While it is helpful to understand more about others' cultures, be careful not to assume that people belong to a specific culture as this, in turn, may lead to difficulties. Ask, rather than assume.

When nonverbal and verbal communication seem to contradict each other, it will damage trust and may escalate conflict.

The best way to be sure that you are not contradicting your words with your body language is to prepare so that what you say reflects how you feel. No matter how good an actor you think you are, emotions show. If you are angry, and you think it would not be helpful to let the other person know, find a way of venting and changing your attitude before you meet. Think about why you do not want the other person to know you are angry. Is there a way of expressing your anger in a different way that would be more productive? Saying you are not angry when you obviously are will make the situation worse. It may help to involve a mediator, coach, or wise friend to help you reframe.

When someone says, "That's fine with me," with sadness in their eyes, unless this feeling is addressed, it will be difficult to resolve the situation. Try responding with a tentative, "I hear you say that it is fine, however it looks like there is something that you aren't happy about. I'd like to know a bit more to see if we could resolve this."

Skills for Listening and Talking

Open Mind

Most people would say that a good listener should be nonjudgmental. In reality, no one can suspend judgment. To say one is not biased is rarely true and often hides prejudice. Rather, be aware of your own judgments and prejudices, and try not to let them affect your behavior. If you deny or bury prejudice, it tends to pop out or silently affect your decision making. It is better to acknowledge to yourself that you dislike someone or disagree with his views. Then, ask yourself, if I liked this person or shared his beliefs, would his behavior be more acceptable? Try and understand what need or fear lurks under your prejudice. Use curiosity to counter any feelings of anger.

Of course, an open mind is also good to have when telling people your story . . . think about how the person hearing it might think of what you say. If you find yourself becoming judgmental or angry, you may need some time out. If this is not possible, take some deep slow breaths and rest your open hands, palms facing up on the desk or on your thighs. Imagine your calmness radiating out and soothing all around you.

Mindfulness

Mindfulness is being present to what is happening right now and giving your whole attention to the person who is speaking. Pay attention to what is said, what is intimated, and what is not said. Listen to the tone of voice, the words the person uses. Watch their body language and facial expressions, if you can see them. Be aware of your own feelings and body language, as an observer, without getting caught up in the emotions. Bring your mind back if it starts to wander.

When you are speaking, be conscious of the other's body language and expression. You may want to clarify or check understanding.

Meditation is a great way of practicing mindfulness, and the more you practice, the easier it will be to do. Mindfulness benefits both the person being listened to intently and the person listening. It creates respect and connection.

You can practice mindfulness in brief moments by focusing on an experience, such as drinking coffee. Engage all your senses, and be aware of your emotions. Do not get distracted by them. When someone speaks to you, practice being mindful by observing the words they use, their expressions, their tone of voice, and their body language.

Questioning

Good questioning is an essential part of good communication. Think about what purpose the question serves and how it should be framed. The best question and style will be the one most appropriate for the situation. Pause for a moment after the person has finished speaking before posing your questions. Think about whether the answer to your question will move toward the desired outcome.

Closed questions which get a Yes or No answer are helpful where there is a clear-cut difference and a decision is needed to move the discussion on.

On the contrary, a closed question limits options and is more likely to shut down conversations. For example, asking, "Do you agree with me about the need for change?" will give you a Yes or No (possibly a "Yes, but" or a "No, but"), whereas, "How do you feel about where the company is at the moment?" will result in a much wider discussion. Closed questions may be leading or threatening.

> I keep six honest serving men (they taught me all I knew); Their names are What and Why and When and How and Where and Who.
>
> Rudyard Kipling

Open questions usually use one of Kipling's "serving-men" and will elicit more information. There is some discussion about whether one should use Why. Taiichi Ohno, former Executive Vice President of Toyota Motor Corporations believed that asking *Why* five times is very helpful in problem solving.

> "Observe the production floor without preconceptions . . . Ask 'why' five times about every matter."

He used the example of a welding robot stopping in the middle of its operation to demonstrate the usefulness of his method, finally arriving at the root cause of the problem through persistent enquiry:

1. **"Why did the robot stop?"** The circuit has overloaded, causing a fuse to blow.
2. **"Why is the circuit overloaded?"** There was insufficient lubrication on the bearings, so they locked up.
3. **"Why was there insufficient lubrication on the bearings?"** The oil pump on the robot is not circulating sufficient oil.
4. **"Why is the pump not circulating sufficient oil?"** The pump intake is clogged with metal shavings.
5. **"Why is the intake clogged with metal shavings?"** Because there is no filter on the pump. (Ohno 2006)

Asking **ourselves** the Five Whys can be very helpful in discovering what the root cause of our anger or disappointment may be. However, used in a conflict or low-trust environment, repeatedly asking the other party Why is likely to be seen as accusation, harassment, or pressure. So many conflict resolution practitioners avoid using Why; instead, using one of the other "honest serving-men": How, what, when, where, and who. For example, instead of "Why did you feel that way?" try "What was behind your feelings?" or "Tell me more."

We need to think whether the additional information gathered is relevant and helpful. While insufficient data may cause us to make wrong assumptions, too much or irrelevant information may obscure or confuse the issue. Do we really need to know everything or is it simply nosiness that is behind a question? Will the question help us come to a resolution or will it side-track us?

Going over and over why something happened can embed negative feelings and escalate the situation. Sometimes, as a mediator, I will say, "Rather than working out what went wrong, let's focus on what we will do to put things right." When one is angry, frightened, or amid conflict, it is not the time to play detective, as the logical brain becomes inefficient under stress. Resolve the issues, then *at a later stage*, work out what can be done to avoid problems in the future.

Appreciative Inquiry (AI), developed by David Cooperrider (Cooperrider 2003) is a very useful tool to use in early stages of disagreement. By recognizing, celebrating, and praising what good you see in the other party, and encouraging them, you are more likely to get helpful responses and willingness to see your point of view. However, if emotions run high and trust is low, the positive questions framed by AI may be seen as ironic or sarcastic. Chapter 11 gives more information on how AI may help prevent conflict from disrupting lives.

Incisive and helpful questions are those which give new perspectives, open minds, and show that one wants to understand the other party. Sometimes, all that is needed is a "How did you feel about that?" or even just "Tell me more."

Paraphrasing and Reflecting

A good way to check whether you understand the other party is to paraphrase or sum up what they have said. It is best to do this in a tentative way, so that if you have misunderstood, the person can correct you. Done properly, it shows that you have been listening and want to understand the other person's perspective. If you can capture the essence of the story, the other person feels heard. Be careful not to add in your judgments or views, but simply to play back your understanding of their story.

Reflecting is mirroring back to the person their words and tone to either clarify or ask a question. Where there is hostility, one should be careful that this is not seen as mocking the other person. It may be safer to express the reflection tentatively, "It sounds like you are very angry about what you heard—would you tell me a bit more about that please?"

Think Before Speaking

Over two and a half thousand years ago, Buddha gave guidelines for right speaking, which are still relevant today. They are echoed in many other great religions and philosophical writings. The five key questions to ask before you speak are:

1. **Is it true?** How sure are you that what you are saying is the truth?
2. **Is what I'm going to say well-intended?** What do I hope to achieve by speaking?
3. **Is it beneficial?** Is what I'm saying constructive?
4. **Is it timely?** Is this the place and time to say this?
5. **Is what I plan to say harsh?** Is there another way to say the same thing?

These five questions are summarized by Figure 7.2.

Is it wanted by the other person? Sometimes, you need to say things the other person does not want to hear, but check first your five questions.

Of course, there are times when we just want to talk without thinking, when we are relaxing or about nonconsequential things. In delicate or difficult situations, it is particularly important to THINK before you speak. Realistically, we will all blurt things out sometimes or misread cues. Chapter 8 covers *ambushes and problems*. Chapter 10 gives tips on *turning disaster into development*.

Figure 7.2 Think Before You Speak

Silence

Silence can be a powerful tool, either to improve rapport or to give both parties time to think. We are often uncomfortable with silence, yet observe the nonverbal clues before breaking it. Rather than leaping in with a solution, it may be more productive to end a silence with a simple "So where do we go from here?"

Putting It into Practice

Communication skills take time and effort. Do not wait until you have a crisis or an argument. Start small, choose one skill, and commit to improving it for a week. For example, you may wish to start with paying attention when listening. Try it when listening to your partner or friends. Note how often you tune out and try and listen as you did when you first met them. Listen carefully to the radio news. Listen to a stranger on a train. Listen to people at work. Actively look for people to listen to, speak less than you usually do. Put down your phone, stop checking e-mail, and really pay attention. Each day, review your performance. What did you do right? What difference did it make? What new information did you gain? Did it change your view on anything or anyone?

Continually practicing communication skills will not only help you in managing conflicts. It will improve productivity, as well as make you more influential and happier.

Check Understanding Chapter 7

- What is the most important communication skill?
- How do you know when someone is really listening to you?
- How important is nonverbal communication?
- List some skills that are important for both listening and speaking.
- Explain the reason that you should ask "why" with caution and how five Why's can be useful in some instances.
- Practice listening intently with undivided attention to someone at least once a day for a week. What did you learn? How did it affect your relationship?

CHAPTER 8

Ambushes and Problems

How to Think on Your Feet and Manage the Moment

Chapters 4–6 describe an ideal process, and Chapter 7 outlines some skills that we can gain to make sure we do it right next time. But what about now? What if you are thrown in at the deep end and have no time to think or learn any new skills?

There are some things that you can do that help the immediate situation. We often firefight and then relax . . . until the next fire. So, just a word of caution, these are emergency procedures. If you do not consider what was the underlying cause, you will continually be firefighting.

In this chapter, I will outline the key principles to help master most situations. This is followed with a few conflict scenarios for you to try and resolve.

Key Principles

Like any martial art, there are some conflict management moves which will work in many conflict situations. With both conflict management skills and martial arts, the effectiveness grows the more you practice. The right mindset is absolutely key for both. The image of the martial arts master in Figure 8.1 is provided to help you remember the key principles of conflict management.

Although we have looked as some of these principles before, in this chapter, we will look at how to apply them when you are thrown in at the deep end.

Manage emotions

Assess the situation

Respect

Trust

Istatements

Asking

Listening

Acknowledgment

Responsibility

Take action

Figure 8.1 Mastering Conflict

Manage Emotions

"I don't have time to bother about how I feel, I need to fix the problem." If you have not read Chapter 2, you will not understand why the right mindset is absolutely essential. If you do not remember or do not have time to read it, let me just recap. Evolution has hardwired the flight/fight/freeze response into us all. This response is triggered when there is a threat or a change and protects us by giving us the mental and physical resources we need to fight, or run away, or freeze. It is a great help if we are faced with a cliff to scale, something to run away from, or someone to fight. It is a big disadvantage if the threat or change needs us to be able to think. Because as well as switching on the adrenaline and power to our muscles, it switches off our brains. So, just when we really, really need to get it right, our logic disappears. If we do not control this response, we are left with anger, fear, or numbness. None of these emotions are particularly helpful in resolving problems, particularly those involving other people.

Our anger will make others feel threatened and they, too, will be under the control of the flight/fight/freeze response. Therefore, conflicts escalate so quickly. When we are in the grip of this survival instinct, all we see is danger, we interpret others' actions as threats, and focus solely on what is best for us. We need to calm and control this response.

Taking the time to do this is essential, as otherwise, we will reduce our chance of managing the conflict successfully. The first thing to do is to breathe slowly and deeply. This slows and steadies your heart rate, and gives you time to assess whether your instinctive physical reaction to the event is the most appropriate.

Mark Goulston, (Goulston 2010) devised a five-step process to control emotions, which he calls "Move yourself from Oh F#@& to OK." The great thing about this process is that the more you practice it, the swifter it becomes. So, in an emergency, you can move from panic mode to solution mode in a few moments.

A critical part of regaining control of emotions is to put words to them. In a study at UCLA (Wolpert 2007), Matthew Lieberman found

"When you put feelings into words, you're activating this prefrontal region and seeing a reduced response in the amygdala," he said. "In the same way you hit the brake when you're driving when you see a yellow light, when you put feelings into words, you seem to be hitting the brakes on your emotional responses."

Goulston uses this information as his basis of moving through the five stages from Oh F#@& to OK, as you name each phase to yourself, you work your brain gradually from panic to control.

Phase	Description	Recommendation
Oh F#@&!	Initial reaction to event, may be fear or anger "Oh F#'&! This is a disaster. I'm screwed, we're all going to die, I can't fix it."	Don't talk to anyone else, acknowledge your feelings and put a name to them. If you are alone, speak out loud. Don't wallow here.
Oh God!	After you've admitted the powerful emotion, you feel a sense of release and start to think of consequences "Oh Hell, this is a huge mess and I'm going to have to fix it."	Breathe slowly and deeply through your nose, ideally with eyes closed and release your emotions.
Oh Jeez!	Now starting to calm and re-center after being blown off course by emotion. "Oh Jeez, there are bound to be things I can do to fix this. It's going to be hard, but I can try."	Keep breathing and labelling what is going on. It may help to repeat the phases yourself. . .OH F!#@!, Oh God, Oh Jeez, Oh Well
Oh Well	Now, start to come to terms with situation. "Oh Well. I'm not going to let this ruin my life/career/day/relationship."	Start to think of what you can do to minimize damage and restore relationships
Okay	Reengaging with the world. "Okay. I'm ready to fix this."	Decide to try. Open eyes, if shut, and act.

Figure 8.2 Oh F#@& to OK Drill (Goulston 2010)

One of the first things we often do is pretend that we are okay when we are not. "No, no, I'm not angry," I say through gritted teeth, getting even angrier because I have to pretend that I am not angry when I am . . . To regain control, we need to stop lying (to ourselves at least).

You may not always start at the Oh F#@& stage. If you are prone to tears (Oh God stage), acknowledge to yourself the urge to cry, rather than fight it.

Assess Situation

If I say, "I can't help it, he just makes me mad when he doesn't tell me about things," I imply that my anger is directly related to the action of not being told. However, in other situations, or with other people in a similar situation, I am not mad. What is the difference? It is the story I tell myself about his action that makes me mad. I may tell myself that he keeps me in the dark because he does not trust me to keep a secret. Or, I think that it is because he wants to hurt me. It is these stories and assumptions that make me mad. If another person was involved, I may tell myself that she forgot, that it was not important or she did not want to trouble me.

So, you need to assess the situation and look at the information you have and the stories you are telling yourself.

> Find the story, Granny Weatherwax always said. She believed that the world was full of story shapes. If you let them, they controlled you. But if you studied them, if you found out about them . . . you could use them, you could change them.
>
> Terry Pratchett, Witches Abroad

One of the most common and least helpful stories in conflict is Karpman's Drama Triangle, consisting of the victim, the rescuer, and the persecutor (see Chapter 2 for more details). If we see ourselves as the victims, blaming others for persecuting us and waiting to be rescued, we lose control of the situation. If we see others as victims and try and ride to the rescue, they may resent it. If we blame others, we take on the persecutor role. In all cases, we become trapped in the triangle.

In assessing the situation, you may feel that now is not the time to handle the situation. Do not ignore it, though; arrange a time and place to address the issues.

Respect

Perceived lack of respect is not only a cause of conflict, but will exacerbate any other problems. Once you have your emotions under control, it will be easier to show respect. No matter how deplorable the behavior, try and separate it from the individual. Try and think of something that you respect about that person. If you do not know the person, think about how you or someone you love would want to be treated in a similar situation. Courtesy and kindness not only makes the other person feel better, but will also make you feel better.

> Swearing doesn't make your argument valid; it just tells the other person you have lost your class and control.
>
> Shannon L. Alder

Showing respect does not have to be elaborate or spelled out. Simply asking permission, ensuring the other person is comfortable, and letting them speak first shows respect. Listening attentively expresses respect. It is better to be over respectful in a conflict situation. Be particularly sensitive when parties are from different cultures or have special needs such as hearing or visual impairment. If in doubt, ask, rather than assume.

The Rose Tinted Glasess Tool (see Chapter 12) helps you see others in a more positive light.

Trust

> The chief lesson I have learned in a long life is that the only way you can make a man trustworthy is to trust him; and the surest way to make him untrustworthy is to distrust him.
>
> Henry L. Stimson

The Trust Equation

$$\text{Trust} = \frac{\text{Credibility} + \text{Reliability} + \text{Intimacy}}{\text{Self-orientation}}$$

Figure 8.3 The Trust Equation (from CH Green)

If you can maintain or restore trust, resolving conflict is much easier. If you lose trust, misunderstandings will increase and conflict will escalate. The book, *Trusted Advisor*, (Maister, Green and Galford 2002) highlights four elements of trust: credibility, reliability, intimacy, and low self-orientation. Figure 8.3 is based on this work.

Credibility is how much people believe you when you speak, reliability is how consistent you are. Intimacy is a feeling of knowing you and feeling safe with you. Self-orientation is low when you think more about others than you do about yourself, and high when you think more of your own interests and concerns than those of others

In a crisis, there are four things that will maintain, build, or restore trust.

1. Speak the truth. Be as honest and as clear as you can. (Credibility)
2. Do what you say you will do. Do not make promises you cannot keep. Be consistent. (Reliability)
3. Be kind. Admit your failings. Help people to feel safe. (Intimacy)
4. Think of others' needs and feelings. (Low self-orientation)

I Statements

Thomas Gordon and his associates researched nondirective methods of achieving positive outcomes. He found that effective I-messages had three essential components. (Adams 2012)

1. A brief blame-free description of the behavior I find unacceptable
2. My feelings
3. The tangible and concrete effect that behavior has on me.

It is hard to disentangle blame when describing how the behavior affects you. Usually, the best way is to see how different statements would

Practical Example

The Late Receptionist

Here are three different ways to describe a situation where the receptionist did not arrive at 8:30 a.m. as agreed and another person had to leave work to cover. Imagine you are the receptionist. How would each of the statements below make you feel?

1. Your lateness yesterday made me so mad. I was in the middle of an important report and the phone rang. Because you weren't there, I had to leave my work and answer the phone. You should be here at 8:30 a.m.
2. I feel very upset when you're not here at 8:30 a.m. to answer the phone because that means I must leave my work to cover for you.
3. Yesterday, I was in the middle of writing an important report when the phone rang and there was no one to answer it. I was annoyed that I had to leave my work to answer the phone as it was after 8:30 a.m. Was there a reason you weren't there?

Which of these statements is most likely to resolve the problem without damaging the working relationship? Can you rephrase it so it is better?

make you feel—if you feel resentful or angry, rather than remorseful, it is likely that there is blame in the statement.

Although it may seem fussy to spend time thinking about how to word a sentence, words can have a big impact. Think of how you reacted to the three different approaches. Remember the trust equation—honesty about your feelings and credibility are important, as well as taking the feelings of others into consideration.

Words are singularly the most powerful force available to humanity. We can choose to use this force constructively with words of encouragement, or destructively using words of despair.

Words have energy and power with the ability to help, to heal, to hinder, to hurt, to harm, to humiliate and to humble.

Yehuda Berg

Asking

Asking someone for their view helps diffuse many conflict situations (see Chapter 7 for more details on questioning). Be genuine in asking and avoid the use of Why. Tone and body language are particularly important if tempers are frayed and the stakes are high.

When someone comes to you with a complaint, try asking them what they feel would put things right. It does not mean that you will do it. If you ask in an appropriate manner, most people will feel better about the situation.

Listening

Listening is one of the most important skills you need to resolve conflict. If you do nothing else, just listen. Attentive listening will not only help you understand what the problem is, it may even be all that is needed. The more someone feels heard, the calmer they become.

Put away your phone, stop doodling, or staring out the window. Lean in, encourage them to speak, ask for more detail. Listen with your body, mind, and heart. Read Listening: Ting in Chapter 7 for more on this vital skill.

Acknowledge

Acknowledge the problem, and their pain as well as yours. Notice the things you agree on as well as the points you differ. Instead of confrontation, try accepting their right to have a different view, build on things you have in common, and compare your view with theirs. Try and see if there is a way that both your needs can be acknowledged.

Responsibility

It can be scary to admit fault, but generally, it will help rather than harm the situation. Taking responsibility for your actions breaks the drama triangle (see Chapter 2) and moves toward resolution. We are each responsible for our own behavior and taking the feelings of others into consideration, but in the end, everyone chooses how they feel about a situation. In every problem, it is helpful to look for what you can control and be responsible for. Some people take too much responsibility and beat themselves up. Others take none, blaming the weather, other people, or bad luck. Be realistic and honest about what is your responsibility.

All negative situations that occur are a combination of three factors: our own actions, the actions of others, and random unpredictable factors. Chapter 10 has a tool to help you assess things realistically.

Take Action

You have calmed things down, you have sorted out what the problem is and agreed a way forward . . . do not stop. Remember the trust equation? You need to follow through and show that you meant what you said. It is always worth ending a conversation with a summary to make sure everyone is clear.

Even if you do not agree on everything, agreeing to disagree or on the next steps that need to be taken should be followed up. Do not leave things hanging.

Challenges

They Will Not Engage

Sometimes, we are willing to change, but others are not. We cannot force others to change. However, we can look at our own behavior and the environment. Ask yourself what you can change, which might influence the other party to engage or change. It might be that there are some hidden obstacles. It might be that they are backed into a corner and cannot see any other options. Is there something that you can do? See Chapter 11 for more information on influencing others to change behavior.

> As a man changes his own nature, so does the attitude of the world change towards him . . .. We need not wait to see what others do.
>
> Mahatma Gandhi

If you have tried everything you can and nothing works, you still have three options. You can accept the situation as it is and be unhappy. You can change your view of the situation and accept it. Or, you can leave or end the relationship. We often say, "I don't have a choice" when we mean that we do not like the consequences. Sometimes, reminding ourselves that we can make another choice, which has worse consequences, helps reconcile us to our current situation.

Extreme Anger

Not only is the Oh F#@& to OK Drill (Goulston 2010) described earlier in this chapter useful for managing your own emotions, but it is also helpful for calming down others (see Figure 8-2). A word of caution—if someone is very angry, they are not thinking straight, and the risk of physical harm is high. Call for help or leave if you feel unable to deal with the situation. Acknowledge the person's anger without blame and offer what you can. "I can see you are very angry about the situation. I would like to help you and to do this I'll need to go to the office. I'll ring you when I get there." Be as truthful as you can, but look after your own safety first; you cannot help anyone if you are injured.

If you feel there is no immediate danger, calm yourself. Calmness is contagious. A few deep breaths and being mindful of the other person as a human being in pain will help you focus. I developed the following tool based on Oh F#@& to OK Drill (Goulston 2010) and *Crucial Confrontations* (Patterson, Grenny and McMillan, et al. 2005).

SALAD Tool

When Anger is in Charge. . .

S. Safety First ensure you are safe. When others become angry, especially if drink or drugs are involved, violence can burst out. If you do not feel safe, leave. **Switch off your anger**, switch on logic. Keep calm. Take a few deep breaths and remind yourself that there is a reason why the person is angry. Think of the best

(Continued)

outcome for this conversation. Keep **silent** to give yourself time to manage your emotions.

A. Acknowledge the person's emotion and **ask** them for their view of the situation. Do not say, "Why are you angry"—they may not know and they may see this as you implying they should not be. Instead, **ask** them to tell you more about how they feel, and what has happened from their point of view.

L. Listen. Let them talk until they stop, then ask if there is anything more. Paraphrase what they have said and check understanding. Help them put words to their emotions, and gradually, gain control so they can thing **logically.**

A. Ask what would make them feel better. **Acknowledge** their right to feel the way they do, even if you do not agree. **Agree** what you can. Be as focused and flexible as possible.

D. Do what you can. Do not promise things you cannot deliver. **Deliver** on any promises you make. Follow up. **Decide** together what is the next step, and if necessary, **document** it.

I Feel Very Hurt

The more you trust someone, the more their broken promise or bad behavior hurts. There is anger at the person, and shame that we trusted them. We lash out, crawl away, or pretend we did not really care anyways.

People are quick to advise. "You shouldn't be so gullible." "Get back at her, promise something and don't deliver. Then she'll see how it feels." "Don't tell anyone, just ignore it." "Tell everyone what he did, and how he treated you."

So, what should you do? There is no one right answer: here are guidelines so you can find the best solution for you.

First, acknowledge your pain. Do not beat yourself up for believing a promise. It may not have been wise, and you may not do it again. However, at the time, it seemed the right choice. Do not add to the pain with blame. Think about what you really need to ease that pain. Think what you really want for the future. Inflicting pain and carrying a grudge rarely make you feel better. Find a way of pouring out your pain, either in a journal or to someone who will listen without judging or advising you.

Second, assess the situation. Does it matter? Is your pain proportionate to what happened? If not, try and figure out what story you are telling yourself about the situation that makes it seem so bad. Check if you have all the facts. Is there something you do not know? What are your options? What is most important to you? Did the promise mean something different to you than to the other person? Is there a time when you broke a promise for a good reason?

Next, choose your path. Remember, you cannot change other people. If you wait for the other person to act, you are allowing someone else to determine your future. They may never apologize, understand, or put things right. You always have a choice, even if it is only how you look at the situation.

Will you give the person another chance? If so, what steps can you take to clarify your expectations and avoid getting hurt again? If you decide not to trust that person again, how will that affect you and your relationships? Will this affect whether you trust others? Remember, intentions behind what people do are usually good, and not trusting anyone will lead to misery. Chapter 10 has a section on forgiveness, and why it can help you heal. Figure 8.4 reminds us of the four "A" s that we need to remember: acknowledge our own pain, assess the situation, accept what cannot be changed, and act.

If you do decide on trying to rebuild trust, it will take time. The other person may also be feeling hurt and may not be ready for your approach.

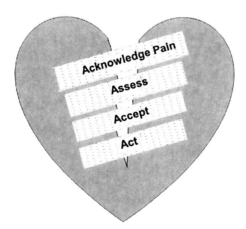

Figure 8.4 When Others Hurt You

They may feel you owe them an apology. If you are thinking, "But it wasn't my fault," then you may need more time or help to heal your own wounds.

Apologizing does not always mean you're wrong and the other person is right. It just means you value your relationship more than your ego.

Mark Matthews.

I'm Wrong

We have all broken promises, sometimes for very good reasons, sometimes for bad ones. What will restore trust?

First, realize that trust takes a long time to build, and moments to demolish. So, do not expect to go back to the same relationship straight away. Take responsibility for what you did without excusing yourself. Try and see it from the other person's point of view.

Then, acknowledge the other person's feeling of pain and anger. Do not offer reasons or justifications first. This may seem unnatural, yet works better. This seems odd, but remember what you thought the last time someone said, "It's not my fault"? Most of us then think "So she thinks it my fault—that's adding insult to injury." When people are in pain, acknowledging the agony is more important than knowing the reason for the pain.

Never ruin an apology with an excuse.

Kimberly Johnson

Once someone recognizes your pain and anger, you are readier to listen to an apology. If reasons or excuses are offered first, the other person feels that we do not value them or understand the consequences of our actions. People need to feel heard before they can listen.

Offer a heartfelt and sincere apology for your actions, not for their feelings. Saying "I'm sorry you are angry" may be interpreted in the other person's mind as "You think it would have been okay if I hadn't been angry about it. So, you are saying it's my fault for being touchy." An apology needs to be like a bandage—bigger than the wound. Whatever you do, do not try and justify your actions at the same time. Ask what the other person needs and what you can do to put things right. Do not promise if you will not deliver. Do not expect that an apology is enough to heal the damage. Words are not usually enough.

Finally, do what you can to put things right. Follow through. The best way to rebuild trust is to be trustworthy. Accept that whatever you do, the other person still may not want to trust you again. You can only be responsible for your actions, not for the feelings of others. But without your actions reflecting your words, others will distrust you. Figure 8.5 reminds us of the three "As" to remember when we are in the wrong.

When we have hurt someone or others have hurt us, the first casualty is trust. In both cases, repairing trust requires similar steps.

When we are physically injured, it inevitably takes longer to heal than it took to inflict the injury. And when we heal, there may be scar tissue and lasting weakness. How well we recover depends on our health at the time of the injury, our approach, the severity of the injury, and the treatment we received. So too with trust. It will take far longer to restore trust than it did to damage it, and things may never be the same.

How can you use the knowledge above and the Trust equation (Figure 8-3 above) in real life? The ABC tool helps remind us what to do when trust is broken.

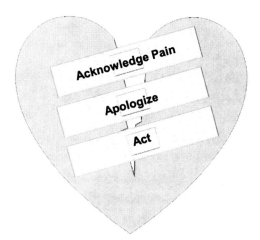

Figure 8.5 When You Are in the Wrong

ABC When Trust is Broken

Like a hand-knitted sweater, trust takes many actions to create, but a single snag can unravel the whole garment. The sooner you act to stop the damage, the better.

A. Acknowledge that something is wrong. **Admit** your part. **Apologize** for any action that hurt the other. **Ask** what you can do to put things right. **Accept** that the other may not be ready to heal or forgive. **Act** as though you can be trusted.

B. Believe the other acted from an unsatisfied need. **Behave** as though you want to repair the relationship. **Build** on common values.

C. Care for the other. Be **consistent**. **Clarify** your intentions. Have **compassion** for yourself and the other involved. **Choose** your path wisely.

To make sure you feel confident in using these skills in a stressful situation, practice them often. Try them out with small things or simulations, adapt your strategies. The next section has some scenarios for you to consider.

A word to the wise, do not practice on other people who are disagreeing. Getting involved in others' conflicts can backfire. Chapter 9 gives some guidelines on whether to step in and how to intervene.

Check Understanding Chapter 8

The examples below are based on real-life situations, with names and circumstances changed to protect confidentiality. There are some questions at the end of each to get you thinking about what could have been done better, and what might help the situation now.

Exercise

Simmering Situation at Simkins

Ed and Ned had worked at Simkins Construction for many years. Both men were skilled artisans and great guys. However, both had short tempers and did not like each other. Several years ago, they had both been away on site, sharing accommodation. Ed had made a sarcastic remark about Ned. Ned had been rumored to have thrown a punch at Ed, but no one reported it, and the management decided to let sleeping dogs lie. Ed was promoted to team leader recently, and Ned resented this as he felt that he had as much experience and skill as Ed. Ed was delighted that he was promoted, and pleased that Ned was not. There was continual low-level aggravation between the two men, and the union were concerned that it was likely to blow up.

A senior manager and the union representative decided to speak with them both. "You are both equally valued by the company and we don't want to lose you. Your continual needling of each other needs to stop before it results in another incident. If that happens one or both of you could lose your job. The new management will not tolerate violence or harassment." Neither of the men was spoken to individually. Both felt that it was the other's fault that they were in trouble with the management. Ned felt annoyed because he felt that he was a victim and that Ed was the firm's favorite. He felt that no one had listened to him. Ed was annoyed that the manager said they were equally valued—he thought that he should have been valued more than Ned because he was a team leader. Management thought that the situation had been sorted and decided to put them both on the same team in the workshop.

Ed was appointed as Ned's direct team leader. Ned was furious. Ed and Ned had different views about how to do certain tasks. The firm accepted both methods. However, as team leader, Ed felt that everyone should do the tasks the way he did. Ned felt this slowed him down and did not give as good a result. Ed insisted that he was the boss

(Continued)

and it should be done the way he wanted. The situation became more and more heated, and Ed stormed off saying he was going to report Ned to management for discipline. Ned was so angry and frustrated that he picked up a tool and flung it in Ed's direction, fortunately missing him. The incident was witnessed by the senior manager, who suspended Ned.

Questions

What could have been done differently by the manager or the union?

What could Ned do to manage the conflict?

What could Ed have done to manage the conflict better?

What does the manager need to do?

What follow-up action should be taken?

Once you have had a go, turn to Chapter 9 or Chapter 10. These chapters give you some additional insights. If you would like more information, e-mail the author at: info@nancyradford.com.

Exercise

Customer Complaint at Cosy Corner Café

Jason was very proud of the café that he had owned and run for 5 years. He had worked hard, building a good reputation for great food and reasonable prices. He only had one member of part-time staff. His teenage daughter, Tina, helped out sometimes. Jason worked long hours and did not make much money. Cosy Corner Café was a bit scruffy, but his regulars told him that it was great just the way it was.

One day, a smartly dressed woman came in and ordered a cup of tea and a scone. Tina took her order, but forgot to bring a knife for the scone. The woman said, "The service is like the surroundings, not great." Tina was upset and retorted, "Well, no one forced you to come in." The customer left and wrote a very critical review in the

(Continued)

local paper. Jason was furious and stormed into the editor's office, threatening to sue the paper.

Questions

What could Tina have done?

What could the customer have done?

What else could Jason do?

What would you do if you were the editor?

Once you have had a go, turn to Chapter 9 or Chapter 10. These chapters give you some additional insights. If you would like more information, e-mail the author at: info@nancyradford.com.

Exercise

Concealed Conflict at Clouds Charity

Chloe and Caroline set up Clouds Charity to help mums with disabled children cope with feelings of isolation and frustration. They had become friends from attending local activities for disabled children. Neither had ever run a business or a charity before, but both were really committed to the cause. Chloe was an inspirational speaker and had lots of great ideas. She loved going out and about talking about the charity and raising funds. She was spontaneous, outgoing, and entrepreneurial. Caroline was very practical and good at keeping track of spending and paperwork. She liked method and organization.

The first year went fairly well, and Clouds started to become better known for its work. Chloe and Caroline complemented each other well. They agreed that they wanted to do more and apply for grants and larger projects. Chloe spoke to the local council at a networking event and discovered they were keen on providing more support to parents of disabled children, and were preparing a tender. Chloe thought this was a great opportunity, but Caroline was concerned that

(Continued)

they did not have the resources or infrastructure to take on a major project like that. However, when she had expressed doubts on previous occasions, Chloe had called her a "negative ninny" and said that she should be more positive and upbeat.

So, Caroline said nothing and prepared the tender submission to set up 3 new regular groups meeting once a month and estimated the costs of the proposal. Chloe was to add the narrative and return the proposal to Caroline to check. The tender was due in at midday on Friday. At 11:00 a.m. on Friday, Chloe gave Caroline the tender to check. Caroline was upset that she did not have time to check the submission carefully and was even more upset to see that Chloe had amended the figures so that there were 5 monthly groups plus a weekly group for the same sum of money. When she raised it with Chloe, Chloe said that she thought Caroline's figures had been overly conservative and that they were unlikely to get the contract unless they offered more.

Caroline was hurt that Chloe had not spoken with her about this earlier. However, she did not feel it would be useful to say anything and sent the tender off.

To Chloe's delight, and Caroline's concern, Clouds were awarded the tender. Chloe saw this as a sign to look for more tenders and intensified her speaking engagements and networking. Caroline began to feel resentful and had more and more to do. The money coming in was not enough to do the work properly. When Caroline tried to raise it with Chloe, Chloe said, "Oh, we will get another tender and then we can employ someone else. Anyways, I'm sure we don't have to go along to every meeting. The groups can do more for themselves." The media loved Clouds and Chloe was often in the paper. Chloe was nominated for an award. Caroline felt that she was doing the lion's share of the work and Chloe was getting the glory, but did not like to say anything because it sounded petty. Caroline felt that trying to do things on a shoestring was against her principles and that her contribution was not valued. So, she resigned as a trustee, much to Chloe's surprise.

(Continued)

Questions

What might have helped avoid some of the issues?

What could Chloe have done to maintain a good relationship?

When should Caroline have spoken up?

Once you have had a go, turn to Chapter 9 or Chapter 10. These chapters give you some additional insights. If you would like more information, e-mail the author at: info@nancyradford.com.

Exercise

Nice or Nasty Neighbors?

Jenny and John Jones moved in next door to Sidney and Sarah Simpson. When the Joneses moved in, Sarah came around with a cake and a bunch of flowers as a welcome to the neighborhood. Jenny and Sarah had a good chat, Sarah talking about her garden and how she loved the peace and quiet of the neighborhood. Jenny about her two boys and how they loved sport. They both thought they were lucky to have good neighbors.

However, one day the Jones boys were playing football outside and kicked the ball into the Smiths' garden. The Smiths were out. The boys thought they would just clamber up the fence to the branch of the tree that grew over the fence, scramble down the tree into the Smith's garden and scramble back with the ball. All went to plan, except that the boys trampled some plants in the Smiths' garden. On the return journey, the youngest jumped down awkwardly into their own garden and hurt his arm. The Joneses rushed out when they heard the wails. Mrs. Jones took the youngest off to hospital. Mr. Jones thought the boys had been swinging on the branch. Worried about getting into trouble, the older boy did not explain further. To stop the boys swinging on the branch, Mr. Jones sawed off the branch at the trunk. He did think that perhaps it made the tree look a bit odd, but he would explain to the Smiths later.

(Continued)

Unfortunately, the Smiths did not return until the Joneses were away on holiday. Sidney and Sarah were appalled to see their favorite tree had been mutilated and that her prize leeks had been trampled. Sarah burst into tears. Sidney was very annoyed and fumed for a week until the Joneses returned from holiday. As soon as they turned in the drive, Sidney marched out to the car and said to Jenny, "You should keep those young hooligans under control. The next time you lot damage my property I am calling the police." Jenny burst into tears. John got angry and said that he had every right to cut off any over-hanging branch. Tempers flared and angry words were exchanged.

Questions

What miscommunication occurred?

What how did this contribute to the conflict?

What could the Joneses have done?

How could the Smiths have handled it differently?

If you were another neighbor, how could you help defuse the situation?

Once you have had a go, turn to Chapter 9 or Chapter 10. These chapters give you some additional insights. If you would like more information, e-mail the author at: info@nancyradford.com.

CHAPTER 9

When Good People Fall Out

You are Not in the Conflict but You Want to Help

How often do you hear the following comments?

> I don't understand why they have fallen out—they are both good people and I don't want to lose either. But I can't stand the atmosphere at work anymore!

> I like both John and Joe but if each has told me if I'm friends with the other one I can't be his friend. I wish I could help them resolve things.

> My neighbors keep trying to drag me into the argument they are having. They both have a point and I don't want to take sides.

This chapter first outlines our instinctive responses to others in conflict. Then, it offers some guidelines on how to decide whether you should intervene. It covers how to work out what would be a helpful approach (with examples) and gives some guidelines. Finally, it will help you know when to call in an expert to manage the conflict.

Instinctive Responses to Others' Conflict

When people fall out, it can poison a work atmosphere, set a bad example for other staff, and cause stress not just to the two people, but also to their manager and to their team. It seems that we all feel "good people" should know how to get along—especially if they are friends or colleagues. It is not just horrible or incompetent people that get stuck in conflict. Conflict is an inevitable part of life and work. The pain of past hurts or unmet needs brings out the worst of all of us. It is hard to watch from the sidelines, so many of us turn away. But what if you are caught in the middle, you have a responsibility to intervene, or you are concerned about the people involved?

If we do not manage our emotions and use our logic and skills, our primitive instincts kick in. We are left with variations of the freeze/flight/fight behavior described in Figure 9.1.

So, why not just use one of these instinctive behaviors? Looking at each in turn will help us see when they might be useful, and the dangers of using them in the wrong situation.

Freeze: Ignoring the Situation

When we ignore a situation where people seem to be in conflict, things do sometimes improve. If the parties involved have a history of arguing and making up, leaving them to it might work. If they continue to work

Freeze	Flight	Fight
Ignoring the situation and act as though there is no conflict	Leave	Punish or exclude one or both of them (if employer, fire one or both)
Talk about it with others but not with anyone who can do anything	Avoid both people	Take sides or make a judgement
Tell parties you don't want to be involved.	Make sure you never see the two of them together	Threaten them

Figure 9.1 When Evolution Controls Our Conflict Management Style

together and the disagreement does not seem to affect their work or their relationship, it may be that the conflict is not as it seems. For example, two workmates become heated when arguing about football, but this does not affect their work or their friendship. Although it may seem safer to ignore a situation if you feel physically unsafe, it is usually wiser to flee. However, if I were in a train bound for Scotland and the two drunks at the other end of the carriage were in a heated argument about whose turn it was to buy the beer, I would try and ignore it if I could not change seats.

However, more often than not, things get worse if conflict is ignored. There are several reasons why ignorance is not usually a great strategy.

First, it sends a message that the conflict is okay or trivial. Those involved may become angry with you or with the organization you represent. Others may imitate them, standards may slip, and work or social interaction becomes affected.

Second, if it seems you are ignorant of the conflict or frightened of it, this may reflect badly on your competence as a manager or your role as a caring friend.

Third, when you think you are ignoring conflict, in reality, you will usually have changed your behavior toward those involved in the conflict. Few of us are such good actors that we can continue to act as normal despite tension and a bad atmosphere.

Finally, as we learned in Chapter 1, conflicts tend to escalate, and this tendency is increased if those involved feel ignored or unheard.

Flight: Avoiding the Conflict

This is like ignoring the situation. We admit that there is conflict, but do not want to get involved. Avoiding conflict may work if those involved are employed on another site or their conflict does not impact on you. There may also be safety issues, which mean avoiding the conflict is the best strategy. Often, fear of conflict and avoidance causes more problems than the actual conflict.

The more we run from conflict, the more it masters us;
The more we try to avoid it, the more it controls us;

The less we fear conflict, the less it confuses us;
The less we deny our differences, the less they divide us.

David Augsburger

Sometimes, flight is the best option. Ask yourself, "Is it safe and sensible to intervene in this conflict? Will my intervention make a difference?" If the answer to either of these questions is a resounding No, then flee or avoid the conflict.

However, if you always flee, you will not develop skills to manage conflict. And there will inevitably come a time when running away is not possible. If you have a responsibility for those in conflict or when the conflict has serious consequences, you need to address the situation.

Fight: Fixing, Judging, or Puniswhing

Forcefully intervening is more likely to escalate or suppress conflict than it is to resolve it. Parents often use this strategy when children are quarrelling, and employers may threaten disciplinary action when employees fall out. This solution will only work if you have the power and authority to enforce. Sometimes, there is a clear judgment call—for example, where one person has broken the law. Other times, both parties behave inappropriately.

Using force to resolve conflict is usually a short-term measure. The parties may seem to have resolved their conflicts as long as the threat of enforcement is there. However, if the dispute has not been resolved, when the threat of enforcement is lifted, the problem recurs. This is seen when peacekeeping forces are sent in. If the underlying issues are not addressed, as soon as the peacekeeping force leaves, the conflict flares again. The other danger of using force is that the parties turn their anger on the person intervening.

This method works if there is a clear judgment call, immediate forceful action is necessary, and you have the power to follow though.

Freeze/flight/fight is a temporary response in the body for a reason. It is effective for reacting to short-term, physically dangerous situations. If continually switched on, in the long term, it will damage the body and no longer effectively protect it. So too with the strategies above. They are short-term strategies which need to be used with care, and supplemented with more logical and long-term strategies.

A Matter of Judgment

This chapter is titled "When Good People Fall Out" to remind you of the helpful view that all of us act in a way that fulfils our needs, not intentionally to hurt others. Although it may be tempting to rush to judgment, we do not know what is behind people's behavior. We tend to be critical of people in conflict, or to assign them roles to fit the drama triangle (see Chapter 1). When we judge, our emotions start to get involved, and logic takes a back seat.

As a nurse in the Emergency Department, I treated a teenager who had been glassed on her hand. Naturally, I saw her as the victim of an attack and condemned the perpetrator. Speaking to a colleague later, I commented, "How horrible to do something like that to a youngster." "Wait a minute," said my colleague, "I've just been treating that man. That teenager attacked him with an axe and he was trying to defend himself. Now he's in intensive care." At that point, we did not know why the girl was attacking the man. He might have tried to rape her. It might have been that that he was protecting someone whom she was attacking. Or, she was protecting someone he had attacked. They may have misinterpreted the other's actions, made the wrong assumption, or acted under the influence of strong emotions, drink, or drugs. They may both have been good people driven to drastic action to meet their needs. Either could be a hero, victim, or perpetrator.

If people act in a way that seems hurtful, we judge them as wanting to cause harm, or at best, stupid. Yet, we know nothing of their intentions, their feelings, and their needs.

> We tend to judge others by their behaviour and ourselves by our intentions.
>
> Albert Schlider

As bystanders, it is easy to judge others when we can see solutions they do not. Remember that anger or fear can trigger switching off logic and cause people to revert to more primitive behaviors. Think about what need is behind people's behavior before assigning negative motives to them. Judgment is instinctive, and it is natural to have your own opinions about what is right and wrong. But before we act on our initial views, it is worth checking whether there is any other interpretation of a situation and whether we have all the information. If we are not careful when we try and help, we end up being sucked into the conflict ourselves. So, the first question is: "Should I intervene?"

Chapter 4 highlighted some questions to ask yourself about whether to speak up or stay silent when you are directly involved in conflict. You may want to refer to this if you find you are or at risk of becoming involved in the conflict. In this chapter, I focus on whether you should intervene when others are in conflict. It is helpful to be aware of your instinctive response to others in conflict. If you instinctively want to act, you may overestimate the risks of doing nothing. If you instinctively flee or freeze, you are more likely to underestimate the risk of doing nothing and exaggerate the consequences of intervening.

If no one holds the "good people" accountable for their behavior, they will continue to fall out. On the contrary, they are threatened, they will seek to justify their behavior by finding fault with each other. That is why getting people to keep a record of instances can be counterproductive.

Before we look at how we should handle conflict between others, we need to know whether we should wade in or walk on.

Wade in or Walk On?

We all like helping people but few of us like to be helped. The first question is to ask whether the disagreement is conflict, potential conflict, or an inconsequential disagreement. Daniel Dana, in his book on work place conflict, holds that there are 4 key components to conflict: interdependence, blame, anger, and consequences to both parties or the business (Dana 2001). I believe that blame and anger are not always obvious in all conflict situations. In *Crucial Conversations*, the researchers highlighted 3 key components: opinions differ, emotions run strong, and the stakes are high. In these cases, conflict is highly likely, so intervening before blame and anger take hold is more effective than waiting for Dana's four components.

So, look at the situation. Are there serious consequences to the relationship, the business, or the individuals? Are emotions hijacking people's logic? Are they on different sides? If the answer to all three is Yes, there

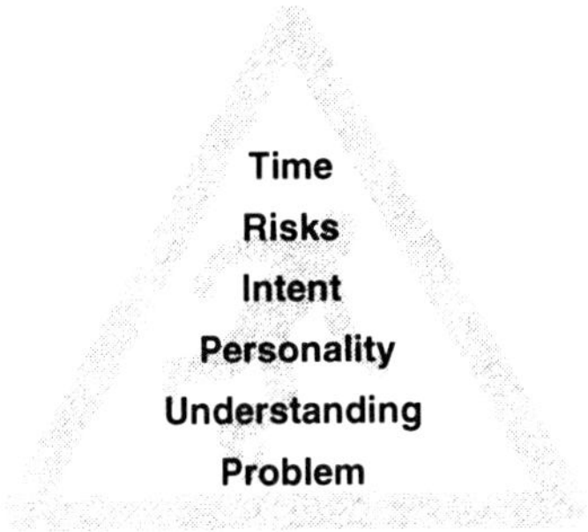

Time
Risks
Intent
Personality
Understanding
Problem

Figure 9.2 Factors to Consider Before Intervening

are still several key factors which should be considered before intervening. If not, our intervention may cause us to trip up, especially in a conflict where we have no obvious direct involvement. Ignoring these factors will potentially worsen the situation. To make it easier to remember these potential hazards, think of TRIP UP as illustrated in Figure 9.2.

It may seem like you do not have time to go through all the factors. In reality, it will take little time to quickly think through the factors and will save a great deal of time, effort, and pain. The more you practice, the more instinctive and easy the process will become. Here is an example which I will use to illustrate the various points. (You can also practice by going through these factors with the scenarios at the end of Chapter 8.)

Practical Example

Problems at Perfect People

Read through the following example and the different options. Which do you think would be best and why? Would there be circumstances that made all of them acceptable?

Claudia is the CEO of Perfect People and comes out of her office one day to hear the Jenny, the Head of Marketing and Joanne, Head of Finance having a heated discussion about budgets. It is an open plan office and it is possible that everyone is listening although they are pretending that they are all absorbed by their work. What do you feel would be the right response from the choice below?

(Continued)

> Claudia decides that this needs urgent action, but doesnot want to embarrass her colleagues in front of staff. She simply says, "Hi, sorry to interrupt your conversation, but I need Joanne's input on an urgent matter." Joanne steps into her office for a discussion, and she later follows up in private with Jenny.
>
> Claudia does not intervene at that stage, but asks Jenny and Joanne to meet with her later that day to discuss the budget.
>
> Claudia does not intervene.
>
> Claudia says, "I'm just leaving, so please use my office for your discussion."
>
> Claudia says, "Please would you both come into my office so we can discuss this issue and let everyone else get on with their work."

Time (and Place)

Before acting, think about the timing and the location. Consider whether now is the best time to intervene or whether to wait until tempers are cooler. Intervening may escalate the problem or it may be necessary to prevent things spiraling out of control. If you intervene in a public conflict, the parties may lose face and turn their anger on you. Generally, it is best to have private conversations with both parties, at a time when individuals are not in the middle of an argument and before positions become hardened. People will be more logical and amenable to accepting help if they are not in the grip of strong emotion or at risk of appearing weak or incompetent. It will depend on the individual and the circumstances.

The right response will depend on the other factors involved. If you were in Claudia's position, you would probably have more knowledge and understanding about the risks, the personalities, and the problem. It might be easier to decide, but sometimes, more information increases the complexity of the decision.

Risks

Realistically assess the risks of doing nothing as well as the dangers of intervening. We each have instinctive ways of reacting (see Chapters 1 and 2 and the start of this book). These will affect how we assess risks.

If Claudia is prone to avoiding conflict, she will focus on the problems that might arise if she intervenes. We may fear the consequences of engaging if we are not in control of our own emotions or lack the skills to manage conflict well and overestimate the risk of speaking up. If Claudia is a fixer, she will highlight the potential disaster that might occur if nothing is done. Some of us enjoy being the hero, rescuing the victim, and punishing the perpetrator. So, we are more likely to ignore the risks of intervening and overestimate our skills.

You may feel that formally filling in a risk assessment before intervention is taking things a bit far. However, if you have mixed feelings and there is time, it can be a helpful exercise. When you have done it once or twice, it will be easier to be accurate in your instinctive judgments.

Figure 9.3 illustrates how to think things through using the example above.

Has the risk assessment changed your view on what might be best? The example above is oversimplified I encourage you to imagine different scenarios and alternative solutions. Risks would change, depending on the intervention used, intent, and personalities, and the issues involved. There is a blank Risk Assessment Form in Chapter 12 should you wish to try this out.

Intent

Examining our own motives before intervening is essential. As we saw in Figure 9.3, some of the risks and benefits are personal. Assessing the situation objectively helps us understand our own motives. Are we intervening to help others or to make ourselves look good? It feels good to be the hero, but sometimes, our help actually takes away another's power or credibility. Ask yourself, "What's the reason I think I should get involved?"

It would be natural for Claudia, in the example earlier, to consider the staff's opinions of her and how staying to discuss the situation might cause problems at home. If Claudia pretended that she was acting purely out of consideration for Jenny and Joanne, it may affect her integrity or result in "leakage." Leakage is when unexpressed emotions "leak" out or are expressed by facial changes or behavior. This causes distrust, confusion, or anger. So, being clear about intent is important.

If Claudia does not intervene			
Positive Consequence	**Chance of this**	**Negative Consequence**	**Chance of this**
Jenny and Joanne stop arguing and agree	10%	Conflict between Jenny and Joanne increases	75%
Staff are busy in their work and do not notice	15%	Staff think that Claudia does not care	30%
Jenny and Joanne feel CEO trusts them to do their job	50%	Claudia looks like she cannot manage senior staff	80%
Jenny and Joanne do not let any confidential info slip	30%	Staff overhear confidential information	60%
Staff feel empowered to be honest and resolve conflicts in their own way	60%	Staff feel it is okay to argue in public and lose their tempers.	60%
Claudia can get home on time	90%	Staff lose respect for senior management	90%
If Claudia intervenes			
Positive Consequence	**Chance of this**	**Negative Consequence**	**Chance of this**
Jenny and Joanne stop arguing and agree	60%	Jenny and Joanne become more defensive and angry	30%
Staff left in peace to work	70%	Staff unsettled and curious	60%
Greater respect for Claudia	75%	Claudia seen as micromanager	30%
Jenny and Joanne appreciate help with managing conflict	Depends on intervention	Jenny and Joanne lose face/ respect from staff	Depends on intervention
Staff feel they can trust Claudia to help manage disagreements	Depends on intervention	Claudia is late home and her family are angry, so problems arise at home	80%

Figure 9.3 Risk Assessment

Stating intent or purpose at the start of a conversation with those in conflict will set the scene. For example, if Claudia stated that she wants to help Joanne and Jenny clarify the issues and find a solution that works for them both, her intervention might be welcome. If she simply tries to stop them arguing, they may both feel resentful.

Personality

Individuals react in widely different ways to the same behavior. That is why we need to think about how the individual in each case will react. A joke to one person could be extremely offensive to another. A gentle hint may be enough for one person to modify his behavior; for another, much more forceful measures may be needed.

If you know the individuals involved, consider your intervention from their point of view. In the first solution of the Perfect People example above, if Jenny was insecure or jealous, she might feel that Joanne and Claudia would conspire against her. If Claudia knew this or the fact that Joanne is likely to tell Jenny a distorted view of what Claudia had said to her, Claudia might choose a different option.

Understanding

Always check your understanding of the situation. What looks like an argument might be a rehearsal for a play or joking between friends. When there is not time to get a full understanding of the situation, avoid making assumptions, talk tentatively, and check frequently that your interpretation of the situation is accurate. Listen to both sides, and try and show your impartiality and respect for both sides. Paraphrasing or reflecting to both parties how the situation looks to you as a third party is often the most helpful thing that you can do. Not only does it check your understanding of the situation, but it also makes the participants feel heard and gives them a new perspective.

Problem

This is linked to understanding what is the real issue. Although in the Perfect People example, it seems to be the budget that Jenny and Joanne are arguing about, it may not be the real problem. Or indeed, it may not be a problem at all; they may be pretending to argue to see people's reactions. It is more likely, as we learned in Chapter 1, there are several underlying causes for conflict.

When emotions run high, it is because people are frightened of losing something or access to something they need is blocked. As well as survival needs (food, air, water, and safety), David Rock (Rock 2009) discovered that there are social threats which evoke the same strong reaction. These are Status, Certainty, Autonomy, Relatedness, and Fairness, given the acronym SCARF. Figure 9.4 gives an overview of these needs and the perceived threats that often trigger conflict.

In the Perfect People example, what threats might affect Jenny and Joanne? Claudia may feel that she is helping save face by inviting one of the participants into her office to discuss the things, but the other may feel that this is unfair.

There are often several threats. In another example, Fred is annoyed that he has not been asked to socialize with colleagues after work. Not only does this threaten his sense of status ("I'm not good enough"), it also affects his sense of connectivity. He may feel it is unfair and it may also make him feel insecure.

As well as the cause of the threat, we need to establish what the issue is. Is it a specific event, the pattern, or the relationship which is causing the threat?

If a colleague interrupts me at a board meeting, I may be angry because I had an important point to make and could not make it on that occasion. On the other hand, it might be that every time I want to make a point,

SCARF

	Description	Threat
Status	Importance in relation to others	The perception of a potential or real reduction in status can trigger a strong threat response
Certainty	Ability to predict the future	The brain is continually trying to predict the near future to keep us safe. Even a small amount of uncertainty generates stress
Autonomy	Control over one's environment	The feeling of having a choice greatly influences the level of stress. When only one option, more stress.
Related	Sense of belonging: Friend or foe?	Feeling alone or amongst enemies or strangers can trigger the flight or fight response
Fairness	Transparency Result reflects action	Unfairness generates a strong threat response. You don't get what you deserve. Lack of transparency erodes trust

Figure 9.4 SCARF Needs and Threats

my colleague interrupts me. Or it might be that I think my colleague does not respect me and this interruption is just one example of his lack of respect. If my manager thinks it is the event, he may feel that it could be resolved by giving me a chance to give my views at the next opportunity. If he thinks that the colleague is making a habit of interrupting, he may speak with the colleague and ask him not to interrupt. However, if it is the relationship that is the problem, neither of these solutions would resolve the situation. It is difficult to know what the problem is sometimes, so it is always advisable to ask the parties to say what they feel is the most important issue. Occasionally, people do not know what the real issue is themselves, so need a bit of probing. A great question is, "So what would put it right?" This helps focus attention on what is really the problem.

Avoid Trip Ups

The tool below will help you assess whether intervention would be a good idea, and give you some ideas about the form of that intervention.

TRIP UP Assessment Tool

An exercise to check whether you should intervene in others' conflicts

Time: Is this the right time and place to intervene? Is there a need for immediate action? Is it a good idea to take action now? Can it wait?

Risks: What are the consequences of doing nothing? What are the chances that there will be negative outcomes from intervening?

Intent: What do I hope to achieve by intervening? What is the ideal outcome? What is the worst thing that could happen? Will my action (lack of action) reflect my intent?

Personality: Do the people involved have any specific issues/sensitivities? What will help them find resolution? What are their triggers? Am I the right person to handle this conflict or is someone else better suited?

(Continued)

Understanding: Do I know what is happening? Do I need more information? Is there someone else who might know more?

P: Problem: What is the cause of the problem? What has triggered the issue? It is the behavior, the pattern, or the relationship that needs fixing?

Worked example

For example, in the toilets of Multiple Manufacturing, manager Jim overhears recent recruit Fred moaning to a colleague that he was not invited to join his teammates for a drink the Friday before, so he is not going to volunteer or do anything he does not have to.

T: It is something that could impact on work, so probably needs to be dealt with sooner than later. Toilets are not really the place to have a private conversation.

R: There is a risk that if nothing is done, Fred will affect productivity or there will be conflict within the team. The manager was not supposed to hear what Fred said, so bringing it up with Fred or his team leader overtly might make Fred angry. The team might be angry if they feel the manager is dictating to them about their social life.

I: Jim does not want to cause more problems. He does not want to micromanage or undermine the team leader. He wants Fred to work well with the team.

P: Jim knows the team leader well. He is a sensible chap and Jim has a chat with each team manager once a day for five or ten minutes.

U: Jim does not know what Fred is like and thinks it might be helpful to know more about the situation before trying to fix things.

P: Jim is not sure whether it is just the lack of invitation, a pattern, or a breakdown in the relationship.

What Jim did

Having considered the various factors, Jim had a chat with Paul, the team manager, asking how Fred had settled in to the team. Paul said that things had gone pretty well, but this week, Fred seemed to be very off-hand and he did not know why. Jim asked if there had been any incidents. Paul could not think. So, Jim asked if the team socialized much after work. "Oh, yeah," says Paul, "We go out every Friday after work." Jim asked if Fred joined in. After the first week, everyone assumed that Fred would just come along, but he did not. Jim's approach made Paul realize that perhaps Fred felt he had to wait to be invited. Later that day, Paul said casually to Fred that he was sorry Fred had not joined them on Friday. Paul said, "After the first week, we don't ask people to come just in case they feel embarrassed to say no. Any time you want to come, just come along. Whether it's just once or twice a year, or never, it doesn't make any difference." Fred's attitude brightened up, and a low-key response averted problems.

Intervening

You have decided to intervene after assessing the pros and cons. What next? Figure 9.5 illustrates some guiding principles and helps us remember to treat both parties equally.

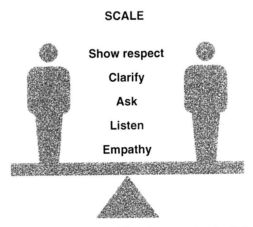

Figure 9.5 SCALE: Guidelines When Intervening in Others' Conflict

Show Respect and Mutual Purpose

If possible, ask permission to have the conversation. In cases where you have a responsibility to resolve the conflict, you may feel this is unnecessary. Even so, giving people an element of choice and respecting their wishes will ease the process. Do not patronize or criticize. Find a common goal that all parties can agree on. It might be to end the hassle, make sure a project gets done on time, or avoid more pain.

You may wish to try and resolve conflicts between your friends. *Definitely* ask permission if you value your friendship. If they agree to discuss the issue, and you want to stay friends with both, you will need to make it very clear that you will not take sides. Sometimes, making peace between friends will mean they become more distant with you. So, you might want to suggest someone else. We often find it easier to speak honestly with strangers because we know we never need to see them again and are less concerned about their opinion of us.

Clarify Issues

First, clarify the issue and the consequences. Going through the Trip Up process (see above) will have highlighted the issues for you. What is the main purpose of intervening? Is it to improve their working relationship? If so, what does that look like? If they are throwing things at each other, you need to ensure safety. Define the issue as factually and specifically as you can. Avoid blame and judgment. Say what you see and the effect it seems to be having on them, you, the organization, or other people.

If possible, do this with both at the same time. If emotions are high, it is often more practical to see each person individually first. If this is the case, be sure that you phrase the message the same way for all parties. Assure them that you will listen to both sides, not as a judge, but as a guide to keep them on track and help clarify their views.

If you are close to both parties or to one of them, this will be difficult. This is where a skilled mediator or conflict coach can help. It is easier to speak freely to neutral professionals than to friends, family, or colleagues because people worry less about their opinions. As a mediator and coach, I have found the chance to talk in a safe environment helps people take responsibility and changes their perspective. Sometimes, this is all that is needed to help people work out their own solution.

Ask

Asking all parties to clarify their views and talk about their situation is the first step. Next, ask questions to find out what really matters to them. Often, parties have similar needs and values. Ask them what is at stake.

> Perhaps the most fundamental way in which the third side can help is to remind the parties of what's really at stake.
>
> William Ury

Focus on what they think would fix things completely and perfectly. Ask them what they could do and what they would do to resolve the issues. Help them to test the reality of any solutions they suggest.

Listen

When tempers are heated, it may be best to see each party separately first. Be sure everyone is clear what is confidential and what can be shared. Be fair and be with each party in turn and for an equivalent amount of time. This will give them a chance to vocalize and put words to their feelings in a safe environment, which will help to calm them down.

Listening is key. When someone feels heard, they start listening to themselves. Reflecting and paraphrasing what they say will help them understand their own actions and judgments.

Listen for things that they might want to share or questions they may want to ask the other person. Check if it is okay to share that with the other person. If you think this might cause a problem, ask, "And how do you think X will react to that?" Alternatively, you may wish to paraphrase or reframe the statement or question and check if it is okay to say that instead.

Empathy

To create an atmosphere of understanding and tolerance, you need to have your own emotions under control. Remember that you are not there to fix things or find a solution, but to support the parties involved to figure out what might work for them. Your role is to ensure that both feel heard and to maintain a safe space for dialogue. Enabling both parties to see a common problem that they can work together to solve, rather than seeing each other as the problem is a big step forward. Do not let your desire to be a hero or find a solution force the pace.

Patience and perseverance are essential. Problems that have been brewing for years will take time to resolve. Yet, it is important not to let people wallow in self-pity or get stuck in blame. Sometimes, a break, some food, or a walk works wonders. It may be that you need to pause, or stop the process. When someone's behavior seems inappropriate, try and think what need is behind it, and how that need could be met.

The children (people) who need love the most will always ask for it in the most unloving ways.

Russel Barkley

When to Bring in an Expert

Sometimes, it is worth using your expertise and knowledge of the disagreeing people to help them resolve their difficulties. In other situations, this can backfire. It can, on occasion, make things worse, or damage your relationship with one or both parties. The three instances below are based on real cases.

Practical Examples

Is a Conflict Specialist Needed?

Disagreeing Directors James and Peter

James and Peter were partners and had built their business up over the past five years. They were now making a comfortable living. A new opportunity beckoned that could bring a great deal more revenue. Further investment was needed, and there was an element of risk. They agreed to bring in a business adviser, Joe. Joe and James had looked at the situation together, while Peter was busy managing other things. James wanted to take the leap and grow the business. This would mean borrowing money. Peter was quite happy with the existing business and was worried about the risks and additional work involved in pursuing the new opportunity

Joe, their business adviser, offered to try and persuade Peter of the benefits. In previous situations, Joe had found that just outlining the benefits to the reluctant partner had done the trick. In this case, it went disastrously wrong.

Joe was not aware that Peter had been reluctant to bring in an adviser in the first place. Peter resented the time and money James spent consulting with Joe. Peter felt that he was being sidelined and was worried about the risks. So, when Joe went in to talk to Peter, the situation deteriorated, resulting in an angry confrontation. Peter became even more resistant and angrier with James. He poured out his resentment and anger, James reacted with his resentment at Peter's "cowardice." Peter asked James to buy him out, and a bitter struggle ensued, ending in the courts.

James then blamed Joe, for damaging his previously good relationship with his partner, Peter. Not only did James fire Joe, but he also advised others not to use Joe's company.

Disagreeing Directors: John and Tony

John and Tony were in a similar situation. Joe, their business adviser, saw there were some sign of potential conflict. They had different needs and perspectives. Although they felt strongly, they found it difficult to express their feelings.

Learning from his previous experience, Joe suggested that both partners talked to an independent facilitator before they decided. Neither would have admitted to any conflict, so describing me as a facilitator, rather than a mediator or conflict coach, was diplomatic. Both agreed that it would be useful to have a private confidential discussion with me.

Tony was pleased to be able to express his reservations about expanding the business and his anger at having to work harder while John was off consulting with Joe. He also talked about the strengths

(Continued)

that they both brought to the business and how he wanted to be more involved in the process. Gentle questioning gave Tony a new perspective on what his concerns and frustrations were. He realized that he had not made his feelings clear to John.

John talked about his frustration that Tony did not seem to want to be involved in the project. He felt that Tony could bring fresh perspective and balance, but Tony seemed to be buried in the day-to-day issues. I explored with him how he could express his views to Tony differently.

Each had the chance to vent his anger and frustration, knowing that it was safe to tell me, as I was impartial and would not be involved in the project. Helping each identify his feelings and his ideal outcome calmed the situation down and clarified the issues. Being listened to made each more ready to listen to the other's views.

I facilitated a joint meeting in which Tony was able to tell John that he wanted to be involved in exploring the options. He said that he needed more help from John with the day-to-day work to free him to contribute to the strategy. John realized that Tony's seeming reluctance was because he felt he had to solve some immediate problems in the business when John was working on the long-term strategy. They talked about how they could work together more effectively. They decided to ask Joe to help them find some short-term solutions that would allow them both to step back and work on strategy.

The end result was good for the partners as the business became stronger. It was good for Joe because both partners were invested in working with him. The partners could work with Joe without embarrassment or previous bad feeling intruding. Because Joe had not heard either of them express negative views about each other, there was no discomfort or feelings of partiality.

There are four factors which indicate that an independent third party may be a better option than a friend or colleague.

1. **High Stakes** If the organization is suffering, if people have started taking sides, or if trust is lost, an impartial expert is more likely

to help find resolution and rebuild relationships. If an attempt at resolution fails, what are the consequences? Using an expert might save you time, money, and heartache.

2. **Connection** If one party is closer to you than another, even if you are scrupulously fair, the other party will feel at a disadvantage. If the parties care about your opinion of them, they are less likely to be honest, and more likely to say what you want to hear. Most of us are reluctant to "air our dirty laundry" with someone we keep seeing as it reminds us of bad times. People involved may worry that someone within their circle will inadvertently let something slip. An outsider is not only safer, but less likely to be biased by history or gossip.

3. **Extreme Emotion** If there seems to be resistance without logic, a history of problems, or likelihood of outbursts, it is best to call in an expert in conflict management, rather than a friend or colleague.

4. **Issues.** Is it straightforward? Is it the tip of the iceberg? Are you likely to be drawn into the conflict if you dig deeper? It may be that other individuals are causing problems or that you are inadvertently exacerbating the conflict. A third party will be able to see things more objectively and shine light on structural and social factors contributing to the conflict. Fresh eyes see things that have faded into the background or taken for granted.

A comment I often hear after a mediation or intervention is, "Thank you so much. You've been great. I hope we don't have to see you again . . . I mean that in a nice way . . ." Once people have concluded a conflict, they really do not want to meet the mediator again as it brings back memories of the difficult times. Apart from expertise, one of the big advantages of using a third party is the sense of closure it brings to those involved. When the dispute resolution is finished, they can draw a line under the past and move on to the future.

Check Understanding Chapter 9

- What is your instinctive reaction when others are arguing?
- What should you consider before you intervene?

- What is the main way a third party can help?
- What is important to remember when intervening?
- What four things suggest that you should call in an expert?
- Think of a situation when colleagues were in dispute. What have you learned that you could have used in that case? What did you learn from what happened?

CHAPTER 10

Turning Disaster into Development

First steps to recovery. Forgiveness. Apologies

The previous chapters have concentrated on helping you to get things right when you are faced with potential or actual conflict. This chapter covers the principles of what to do when things have gone wrong, how to apologize, why forgiveness is important, and how to make sure we learn from our mistakes.

First Steps

Just as the three "Rs" are the basis of learning, there are three key "Rs" in recovering a conflict situation that has gone wrong: Recognition, Responsibility, and Restoration. If you find that you are caught in the whirlpool of conflict and feel like you are being dragged down, they provide a life belt, as in Figure 10.1.

Recognition

When things start going wrong, it seems that they can spiral out of control very quickly. One thing after another seems to happen. There are two early indicators that things are not going well for you: denial and emotional hijack. Catch yourself in time and it is easier to turn the situation around.

Figure 10.1 Life belt for Those Caught in the Conflict Whirlpool

Our first instinct is to deny there is a problem. We reassure our-selves and everyone else that things are just fine, it will all blow over. That adds inner conflict to our problems, as a little voice inside is say-ing, "You're making a mess of it," and we waste a lot of time trying to drown it out.

Learn to recognize the signs of emotional hijack as these may appear even before you are aware things are going wrong. Are you raising your voice? Is your heart rate increasing? Do you feel sick? Are you sitting with arms crossed?

When you recognize the conversation or situation is deteriorating or in stalemate, William Ury (W. Ury 1991) suggests "going to the balcony." This means mentally or physically stepping out of the conflict for a period to calm down and reassess. It may be advisable to arrange a strategic delay until everyone has time to recalibrate. If this is not possible, ask for a moment or two to compose yourself. Even just a few moments thinking of something else or deep breathing will help calm you. Another good alternative is to go for a walk. It is hard to argue when walking and physical exercise is good at relieving tension.

If you have time to express negative emotions in a safe place, this will help enormously. You could write them down, speak with a coach or anyone who will listen in confidence without judgment or advice. Figure 8-2 provides a useful tool, and Chapter 3 has several other tools to help you manage your emotions and restore logical thinking.

It is also important to be aware of our own limitations. We can only do our best. We cannot change others and some situations are beyond our control. It is critical to recognize when we should persevere, when we should call in expert help (see Chapter 9), and when to walk away.

Responsibility

When things start to go wrong, some of us leap to the rescue. Others wait and see if anyone else will intervene, and some hang back. Any one of these responses may be appropriate. So, how do we know what is our responsibility? The Responsibility Pie Chart Tool can help you work this out. This exercise has been attributed to various authors and is widely used in Cognitive Behavior Therapy when people are stuck in blaming others or themselves disproportionately. I first learned of it through the Bounce Back resources, based on research by educational psychologists (Noble and McGrath 2008). A Responsibility Pie Chart is based on the principle that all negative situations can be said to occur as a result of the combination of three factors: our own actions, the action of others, and random unpredictable things. Creating a pie chart every time something goes wrong would be over the top. However, by assessing the proportionate responsibility of the different factors, we gain a more objective picture of the situation and possible options for resolution. It is useful not just for learning from mistakes, but also, for highlighting solutions and motivating us to take restorative action.

Responsibility Pie Chart Tool

Negative events are due to a combination of three types of factors: our own actions, the actions of others, and random unpredictable things.

Start by thinking of a negative event that happened to you recently. Draw a pie chart illustrating the three factors without thinking.

Now, list all the reasons that contributed to the result. Try and put down everything that contributed to the event, however small. (See the following worked example for further guidance on how to use this tool.) You must always allocate some responsibility to yourself, as your choices contributed to the situation. It is useful to try and avoid the words "blame" and "fault," instead asking questions such as:

- How much was . . . responsible for what happened?
- What was this due to . . . ?
- What made this happen . . . ?
- How much does . . . explain what happened?

Continued

Starting with the least important factor, give each factor a percentage and group them into the three categories mentioned earlier.

Add up the categories and draw your pie chart again.

Compare the two.

What can you learn about yourself from the way you apportion responsibility?

What would you do differently next time?

Worked Example

Mary and Dennis were business partners in a bakery as well as spouses. Mary managed the bakers and Dennis ran the retail shop. One day, the flour delivery was late, so not all the varieties of loaves were ready, despite the bakers rushing like mad to try and get things done. They were so busy baking that Mary had not told Dennis why they were late. When a customer complained that her favorite loaf was not ready, Dennis said "So sorry, I'll be remonstrating with the bakers about their idleness." Mary overheard this and was furious. When Dennis came back into the oven room, she snapped "You are one to talk about idleness. You just get to chat away to the customers. We're the ones who have to rush around doing all the work. You get all the praise and blame us when things go wrong. You have no idea of the problems we solve while you sit out there chatting." Dennis thought she was overreacting and told her so, defending himself and maintaining that if it was not for his sales ability there would not be a business . . . things went downhill from there.

The two pie charts below show the change in Mary's thinking. Initially, she thought that she had little responsibility for the argument, blaming it on mainly on Dennis. When she asked herself the objective questions, she recognized the role that **chance** had played in the customer coming in when they had, the reason for the delivery being late, and **her own responsibility** for letting Dennis know what was happening and losing her temper.

Continued

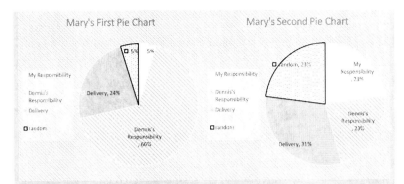

Figure 10.2 Worked Example of Pie Chart Exercise

How do you think this altered perspective could help Mary recover from the situation? Does recognizing your responsibility in a negative situation provide new ideas on how to improve or resolve the situation?

There is a fine line between responsibility and blame. To tell the difference, notice the emotions involved. Shame and anger usually accompany blame. Feeling responsible for something will make you want to put things right. Being blamed for something will make you feel defensive and trigger the instinctive flight/fight/freeze response. When trying to establish responsibility with others, be careful with the questions you ask and the tone of voice to avoid blame or excuses.

Restoration

The final R is restoration. Knowing what went wrong and learning from it is great. Too often, we move swiftly on without thinking about what we can do to put things right. It is uncomfortable to be in a conflict situation, particularly if things have gone wrong. Yet, ignoring it, running away, or blaming others will not work.

> You can't talk your way out of something you behaved your way into. You have to behave your way out of it.
>
> Doug Conant

If things have gone wrong, something needs to be done. You can either wait for someone else to act or you can act. Perhaps all you can do is to accept the situation and change your attitude. Often, there is something concrete that you can do to make the situation better. Even small kindnesses make a difference. Ask the other party what they need to restore their faith in you or to rebuild trust.

One of the best ways to restore others' trust in you is to show trust in them.

> The chief lesson I have learned in a long life is that the only way you can make a man trustworthy is to trust him; and the surest way to make him untrustworthy is to distrust him. Henry L. Stimson

Stephen MR Covey maintains that integrity, intent, capability, and results are the "Four Cores of Credibility" (S. M. Covey 2006) needed for trust. All are needed to restore a healthy relationship. **Integrity** means believing that the other person will behave in a way consistent with their words and their values are congruent with yours. Both parties believe that the other's **intent** is good and that their goals are similar. Each party trusts that the other party is **capable** of following through on promises and upholding values. If the expected goals and actions actually happen (**results**), this creates the fourth pillar of a good and stable relationship. (See also the section on trust in Chapter 8 or Chapter 12 for the tool "ABC When Trust Is Broken."

Apologizing

Before you apologize, you need to be sure that you have "put your own oxygen mask on first" by handling your own feelings of hurt or anger. Otherwise, you may find the right words for your apology, but your unresolved feelings leak out through your body language and tone. The other person will see the dissonance between what you say and your body language, and think your apology is insincere. An insincere apology makes things worse, rather than better.

A good apology is like the first two steps of recovery. First, you **recognize** that something is wrong and accept **responsibility** for your actions. However, for an apology to be effective, you also must **realize** and acknowledge the pain the other person feels. You also need to show **remorse** for your actions. When a relationship starts to unravel, stitching it back together takes longer than it took to inflict the damage. An apology can provide a start.

The SEAM Apology Tool below provides guidance on how to frame an effective apology.

SEAM Apology Tool

For an apology to be effective, it must come from the heart and be sincere. The sooner an apology is offered, the better. If the person is very hurt or angry, you may have to offer the apology more than once. The longer you leave, the less effective it will be, and the harder it will be to apologize. No matter how good an actor you are, if you are defensive or angry, your tone and body language will betray you. So not only do you need to get the words right, you need to get the feelings right. SEAM reminds us of what makes a good apology that will help stitch relationships back together.

- **Seek perspective** Try and see the situation from the other person's point of view. How would your actions have seemed? What are the benefits of restoring your relationship with this person? What have you lost by damaging the relationship? Think about the person's characteristics that attract you and the good things they have done for you. Do not try and justify your actions. Be clear about your motives.
- **Express remorse.** An apology is not a justification of your actions. Start with "I'm sorry I . . . (insert action or behavior). I feel ashamed of myself." A real apology acknowledges the validity of the feelings or values of the other person. Saying "I'm sorry you were upset by my comment. It was just a joke" implies that the other person cannot take a joke. It would be better to

say, "I'm sorry you were upset by my comment. I should have realized it could be hurtful."

- **Admit responsibility.** Taking responsibility means not only admitting that your behavior was wrong, but also showing that you understand the implications of the behavior. Do not offer excuses or reasons for your behavior until the other person asks for them.

Imagine you are angry for sitting waiting in a bar for a partner to turn up. Compare "Sorry I'm late for our date, but I got held up in traffic" with "I'm so sorry I'm late. I feel bad that you had to wait so long for me. I really wanted to be here on time so we could have lots of time together. I should have allowed more time for traffic on a Friday."

- **Make amends.** The most wonderful apology is meaningless if you do not offer to make amends, and you do not follow through. The other person needs to be reassured that you have recognized the error of your ways, you want to put things right and that you will not do it again. Ask what you can do and follow through. Do not make promises you cannot keep. Explain how you plan to change your behavior in the future. The follow through is essential. The more you keep your word, the more effective your apologies will be.

If you do not invest in an apology, it is not likely to be effective. An apology may not be enough. The most persuasive apologies involve sacrifice: either time, ego, vulnerability, or goods. Sometimes, our apologies are ignored or rejected.

If someone refuses to forgive us, it can be very painful. When we apologize, we feel especially vulnerable, and rejection hurts. The tendency then is to lash out. "I've said sorry, what more do you want?" We then start justifying our actions and finding fault. This will negate our apology, exacerbate the conflict, and damage the relationship.

How can you avoid reacting in a way that makes things worse? First, be prepared that the other person may not be ready to listen or to forgive.

Second, remind yourself that you may not fully understand the other person's pain. Think of how much pain they must be in to reject your apology. It will give you an insight into some of the hurt they are suffering.

> If we could read the secret history of our enemies, we should find in each man's life sorrow and suffering enough to disarm all hostility.
> Henry Wadsworth Longfellow

It might give you some ideas of how to apologize in a different way. Finally, see this as your chance to practice forgiving the other person as you would like them to forgive you.

> As long as you don't forgive, who and whatever it is will occupy rent-free space in your mind.
>
> Isabelle Holland

Rebuilding a relationship requires both parties. It may be that the other person does not want to rebuild it.

> Rebuilding trust when it's been broken is not dependent only on the person who has broken it, or how many times they can prove they are honest. It depends on the person who has decided not to trust anymore. Though they may be totally justified in their decision not to trust, as long as they choose not to, the relationship has no hope of survival and should be ended. If or when they decide to trust again, there is hope reborn.
>
> Doe Zantamata

When you have done all you can, sometimes, you must accept that the relationship has come to an end. To be able to move on, you need to do this with forgiveness, rather than resentment.

Forgiveness

For thousands of years, mercy and forgiveness have regarded as virtues, helping to heal and build civilized societies. Research has found that forgiving others actually benefits us as much as, if not more than, those we forgive (Toussaint, Owen and Cheadle 2012).

So, what is forgiveness?

> a conscious, deliberate decision to release feelings of resentment or vengeance toward a person or group who has harmed you, regardless of whether they actually deserve your forgiveness. (Greater Good Berkeley Forgiveness n.d.)

Forgiveness is not glossing over the hurt nor condoning wrongdoing. It does not release others from their accountability nor does it mean we forget what has happened. It enables the forgiver to let go of deeply held resentments and hurt so that healing can take place and the person can move on. When I forgive, I am saying "What has been done to me is wrong, yet I will not let the other's actions define me and constrict me." Forgiveness means deciding to free ourselves from the anger and blame and concentrate on the positives and the future.

Psychology Professor Everett Worthington not only researches forgiveness, but also practiced it by forgiving those who murdered his mother. He teaches forgiveness using the acronym REACH (Worthington 2016), as shown in Figure 10.3.

As we have learned before, to control emotions and to heal, we need to acknowledge the pain and recognize the emotion. So, the first step is to **Recall** the hurt, recognize that holding on to the pain and desire for revenge will hurt you more. Holding on to your hurt and anger is giving the other person power over your mind. It is giving away your control over your thoughts.

Figure 10.3 REACH (from Worthington 2016)

Holding on to anger is like grasping a hot coal with the intent to throw it at someone—you are the one getting burned.

Buddha

Empathize with the people who inflicted the harm. What need or emotion might have caused them to behave that way? A victim who went through the restorative justice process lost her fear when she found out more about the perpetrator. The young man who had damaged her car had not done it from a desire to hurt her, but because he was frustrated and angry with his life. He did not understand the impact of his actions. She said, "I went from being scared to feeling sorry for him."

Decide to give forgiveness as an **Altruistic** gift. We know how wonderful it felt when someone forgave us. This is our chance to restore the balance.

Forgiveness is not temporary; we need to make a **Commitment** that will help it last. A public commitment or a note to yourself that you have forgiven the person will increase the chance of forgiveness continuing.

It is important to commit because it helps us **Hold** onto forgiveness when emotions start to take over.

So, you do not need an apology to forgive someone, as it is not about helping them to feel better (although it usually will), but about letting go of your anger and hurt.

Forgiveness undoes our own hatred and frees us from a troubled past.

Christopher Peterson

Here is an exercise if you are struggling with forgiveness.

Forgiveness Tool 1 Letters

Write a letter to the person who hurt you (which you are not going to send), recalling the incident, telling them of the impact it had on you. Pour your heart out.

Now, imagine how you would like that person to respond to your hurt. Write a letter as though the other person was responding to your pain with understanding and empathy. Describe the possible reasons

Continued

behind the behavior. Say what could be done to ease your pain. Write of the problems from the other person's point of view.

Now, read the letter. Allow yourself to feel compassion and understanding, and write back describing what you feel and what forgiveness means to you.

Remind yourself that forgiveness is your choice and your gift. Think of the peace it will bring you and the benefits.

Now, burn all the letters.

If you have decided to forgive, write a reminder to do something that will show your forgiveness. If you have not decided to forgive, you may find talking to an impartial third party helpful.

Forgiveness Tool 2 Chairs

Find a private place and set up three chairs.

Imagine the person who wronged you is sitting in the other chair. Speak to him/her honestly and clearly about the impact of his/her behavior on you. Tell them how you feel, what hurts most, and what you would like them to do. Once you have poured out your heart and expressed all your emotions, take a deep breath.

Change chairs. Now, imagine you are the other person and there is an imaginary you sitting opposite. Talk back to the imaginary you in a way that helps you see why the other person might have behaved the way he/she did. What could make people behave that way? What need might have been driving the behavior?

Pause, breathe, and change chairs so that you are sitting in the third chair. Try and see the situation as an impartial third party. Help reconcile the two views. Ask, what next?

If you have decided to forgive, write a reminder to do something that will show your forgiveness.

If you cannot forgive, you may find talking to an expert third party helps you to move on.

A note of caution about sending a forgiveness message or telling others you have forgiven them. If this is done before the person has apologized, it might appear accusatory. Peterson (Peterson 2006) describes asking his students to write a "forgiveness letter." After the exercise, the students discussed whether to send the letters. All but one student decided not to, as they felt it might backfire. The one student who sent the letter still has not been forgiven for writing it.

Learning

No matter how disastrous an event, there are always things we can learn from it. Rather than beat yourself up about the mistakes that you made, or blaming others for their attitudes, think about what you could do differently next time. Try and see every conflict as an opportunity to learn something. For some guidance on how to learn from negative events see The Sad to Glad Tool in Chapter 12.

Check Understanding Chapter 10

- What three Rs can help you when you are caught in the conflict whirlpool?
- What are the advantages and disadvantages of using a Responsibility Pie Chart?
- What are the four components of an effective apology?
- Who does forgiveness help most and why?
- Describe how REACH helps you forgive.
- Think of a situation when someone hurt you. If they apologized, was it effective? Did you forgive them? How did it make you feel?

CHAPTER 11

Prevention

Avoiding the Conflict Whirlpool
What influences people. Boundaries

Conflict is inevitable. Although you cannot avoid conflict, you can avoid being sucked into a damaging whirlpool spiraling out of control. You can limit the damage, prevent unnecessary conflict, and create an environment which encourages healthy practices.

Six Sources of Influence

Understanding what influences people's behavior gives us deeper insights into their reasoning and ways to implement lasting positive change. A study into people who had success in areas which others had failed resulted in some very interesting findings. (Patterson, Grenny, et al. 2008). We generally attribute noncompliance to our wishes to the other person's bad intentions. Sometimes, we know or guess that compliance will not bring them the rewards they want. Hence, when others do not engage, we try and increase their motivation to do so by threatening or cajoling to increase their personal motivation. Or we may make changes to rules or remuneration to mold people to the desired behavior. What this research discovered was that change based only on personal motivation or structural rewards did not last. They learned that

> to create long-term, sustainable positive results you need to change hearts, minds, and operations, as opposed to simply managing people through tasks or inspiring short-term, specific actions. (Patterson, Grenny, et al. 2008)

By studying instances where long-term change of previously resistant behaviors had occurred, the team identified a winning solution. The organizations examined varied from one that reduced reoffending, to a campaign to improve hand washing in hospitals and getting rid of guinea worm in Africa. The research found that success was down to identifying critical behaviors, and then, addressing them using as many of sources of influence as possible. They identified six key sources of influence, as shown in Figure 11.1.

Most strategies for change use either personal motivation or structural motivation. The projects with the least conflict and the most lasting change used at least four, if not all six, sources of influence.

Personal Motivation

This source is the one we usually choose first. We tell ourselves that others do not want to change. We think they lack drive or compassion. If we focus on this area, we are likely to become judgmental and blame the other person. This is unlikely to improve the situation, and often, makes it worse. This may increase tensions and misunderstanding, leading to conflict.

Personal Ability

Thinking about this aspect may provide a real breakthrough. The person's behavior may be due to an inability to do anything else. My

Area	Motivation	Ability
Personal	What is wanted? What is hated? Do I enjoy it?	What skills do I need? Am I personally able?
Social	Do others motivate me to do it or discourage me from it?	Do others enable me or disempower me?
Structural	Do things/ surroundings motivate me or discourage me	Do things/surroundings make me more or less able to change?

Figure 11.1 Six Sources of Influence (from the book, Influencer 2008)

brother-in-law, Peter, who is blind tells the story of bumping into a man on the street who reacted angrily because he thought Peter had purposely jostled him or was just rude. Imagine the man's embarrassment as he ended his tirade with "What's the matter with you, are you blind or something?" and Peter answered, "As a matter of fact, I am." No matter how motivated the person is to change behavior, if the skills or ability is absent, change cannot occur.

Social Motivation

Peer pressure is not just important in your teens. Our family, friends (online and off), and our culture exert huge pressures on us. We often are unaware of these until we meet people whose values and behavior differ from ours. For example, belching loudly after a meal is considered very polite in some cultures and vulgar in others. People want to belong and will even sacrifice self-interest to be accepted by their "tribe."

Social Ability

I worked in a deprived area of Britain, where there were six generations of widespread unemployment. Parents did not know how to help their children look for employment and were reluctant to raise hopes that might be dashed. It was not that they did not want their children to work, it was they did not know how to help them to achieve this.

Structural Motivation

Rewards and punishment have significant effect on behavior. This is where we often turn when personal motivation seems lacking. Laws are passed, procedures implemented, and incentives put in place. For example, to deter shoplifting, many stores will have signs warning of penalties and obvious security personnel. However, if enforcement is removed, the behavior recurs. Bonuses become expected. The effect of incentives wear off. Although changes in law (for example the seatbelt rule and anti-smoking legislation) can gradually change behavior, they can create a backlash. If rules are perceived as unfair, this may cause more problems.

Structural Ability

This is equally important to reward and punishment. As well as the threats of punishment, to reduce shoplifting, shops look at ways of making theft difficult by putting valuable items behind glass or linked to alarms. Ex-offenders are helped to find jobs to ensure they have funds without turning to theft.

The Influencer Tool below guides you through the six sources of influence. The researchers found that the more sources you tapped into, the more chance of achieving lasting change.

As shown in earlier chapters, understanding why we and others behave in certain ways not only makes us more tolerant, but also helps us find ways of avoiding unnecessary conflict when implementing change.

Influencer Tool

Choose a specific instance of resistant (or wrong in your eyes) behavior. Answering the questions below will help you find reasons for the resistant behavior and give you insights into what (if anything) can be done to change others' behavior without conflict. You may reassess your views on the behavior. Work through the model and ask yourself the questions. (There is a blank form in Chapter 12.)

Source 1 Personal Motivation: Do they want to engage in the behavior? Do they enjoy it? What would make them want to behave in the desired way?

Source 2 – Personal Ability – Do they know the consequences and benefits? Do they have the skills needed to behave in the desired way? What strengths do they have? What do they need?

Source 3 – Social Motivation – Are other people encouraging the right behavior and discouraging the wrong behavior? What could be done to create positive peer pressure?

Source 4 – Social Ability – Are friends able to provide the help, information, and/or resources required? What can family or other social groups provide?

(Continued)

Source 5 – Structural Motivation – Are rewards, pay, promotions, performance reviews, perks, or costs encouraging the right behaviors? Does the unwanted behavior incur any penalty or negative consequence?

Source 6 – Structural Ability – Are there enough cues to stay on course? Does the environment (tools, facilities, information, reports, proximity to others, policies) enable the right behavior? What might make it harder to do the wrong thing?

What ideas has this given you? Has it changed your views in any way?

Focus on Positives

Conflict escalates and causes damage when we focus on the negatives and points on which we disagree. While being realistic and recognizing faults is important in resolving problems, we should also look for the good on which to build. Negative comments and criticism create defensiveness or aggression. We need to learn ways to improve ourselves, our relationships, and our performance, which are constructive rather than destructive. The common grievance and disciplinary procedures are based on recording instances of negative behavior. This often exacerbates the problem. Appreciative Inquiry is a method of looking at the positives in an organization, and provides a different way of looking at a potential conflict or difficult person. The four foundational questions in Appreciative Inquiry are:

- Describe a high-point experience in your organization, a time when you were most alive and engaged.
- Without being modest, what is it that you value most about yourself, your work, and your organization?
- What are the core factors that give life to your organization, without which the organization would cease to exist?
- What three wishes do you have now to enhance the health and vitality of your organization?

Translating these questions so that they could apply to a relationship produced the Rose-Tinted Glasses Tool. Use of this tool gives a different view and may help restore a more balanced perspective.

Rose-Tinted Glasses Tool

Think of the parties in the conflict in terms of their work, their personalities, and their contribution.

- Describe a good time that you had with the other person, or something that they did which helped you, or a contribution that you valued.
- Recollect something that you did for them that made you feel good. Was there a joint achievement of which you are proud?
- What do you (did you) particularly value about the person or the relationship? What benefits did the relationship bring you? What were the key factors in the relationship?
- What three wishes do you have for the relationship going forward? What could you do to bring them into existence?

We rarely praise enough, and when we do, we are not specific. One of the most common underlying causes of conflict is feeling unappreciated and undervalued. Studies of the effect of positive and negative interactions show that it takes between three to five positive interactions to counteract one negative one (Rath and Clifton 2004). By encouraging more positive interactions, we will create more resilient individuals who are better able to manage their emotions.

Simple kindnesses can make a huge difference. Helping a colleague tidy up, asking after their family, or buying coffee for the team may not seem important, but will build stronger relationships and reduce unnecessary conflict. If you know, like, and trust someone, you are more likely to discuss differences amicably.

Positive reinforcement changes behavior for the better, while criticism stabilizes negative behaviors and blocks change.

Virginia Pearce

When we look for the positive in others, we reduce some of our fear. Reducing fear will lessen the instinctive aggression and defensiveness.

> The boulder in the path to resolving conflict is fear – fear that the other side of the conflict is up to no good and any concessions we make will be interpreted as a sign of weakness and invite further aggression. The fear comes from our hardwired, primitive and un-differentiated response to stress that we unconsciously experience as a threat to our very existence. . . . complicating things is the fact that our self is usually left at home and we show up consumed by our largely imagined notions of who we are dealing with and what they are thinking. And we often imagine that the other side is Beelzebub and we are angels.
>
> Roger C Benson

By focusing on the good in others and in ourselves, we decrease the chance of destructive behavior. When we find common goals and values, we increase the chance that differences bring diversity, rather than division.

Why Boundaries are Important

People often describe mediators as those who break down walls and build bridges. So, why do I say that boundaries are important in preventing conflict? One of the most common causes of conflict is when someone crosses another's boundary. We create boundaries to keep us and our valuables safe. Think of the walls around your house. If a door is left open and someone unknown wanders in, most people will feel threatened. If it is someone we know, we might not mind—or we may still expect them to ask permission. We all have invisible trip wires around our personal space, which is show how close others can come without it being uncomfortable. This also extends to behaviors and values. These vary with culture and upbringing. Our boundaries seem logical and sensible to us—so much a part of who we are that, at times, we are not even aware of them.

> We don't see the world the way it is, we see the world the way we are.
>
> Anais Nin

Sometimes, our boundaries are crossed because others are not aware of them, or they do not understand their importance. Or, they may not understand the consequences. Occasionally, we do not realize where our boundaries are until someone has crossed them. We tend to think that everyone has the same needs and desires as we do. We have expectations that others will respect our boundaries, as we do theirs. When they are not met, we react badly.

> When we fail to set boundaries and hold people accountable, we feel used and mistreated.
>
> Brené Brown

Sometimes, the fear of conflict stops us expressing our concerns, establishing limits, or preventing others from trespassing. Inevitably, this will lead to problems—either we will become downtrodden or explode. So, having clear boundaries, which everyone can understand helps prevent unnecessary conflict and pain. However, limiting other people's freedom by doing this can also create disagreement and aggravation.

How to Set and Maintain Boundaries

So, how can you set clear boundaries and maintain them without causing problems?

> When trying to teach someone a boundary, they learn less from the enforcement of the boundary and more from the way the boundary was established.
>
> Bryant H. McGill

The first step is to set your boundaries and know what they are. Self-knowledge is key.

Know Yourself

We know that someone has crossed the line when we feel uncomfortable, frightened, or angry. Recognizing what triggers these feelings will illuminate why we have the boundary and help us decide how to respond. Figure 9.4 illustrates common areas where people create boundaries to prevent loss. For example, if status is important to John, comments about how his car is not as good as Peter's might make him angry, yet the same comment might not offend others. John's anger is not necessarily about the comment, but because it makes him feel belittled. It may be that he links the comment with a painful experience.

> Boundaries represent awareness, knowing what the limits are and then respecting those limits.
>
> David W. Earle

In a workshop I ran, one of the exercises included coloring in a picture. A fifty-year-old man became offended at being asked to do this. When we talked about it later, it turned out that it reminded him of his very unhappy time at primary school. Once he realized that this fear of being hurt was behind his reaction, he was happy to "push his comfort zone."

Awareness of your own triggers is helpful not only in establishing what your boundaries are, but also exploring whether they are useful. Are they necessary? What are they protecting? What would make if okay for someone to cross them? Is there a need to make them more obvious?

Clarify Expectations

If there is something that triggers extreme emotion in you, and you want people to respect that, you need to tell them. Birds often fly into glass doors because they do not see them. Do not expect people to know what you want or do not want. Not everyone thinks like you. Letting people know what is acceptable or unacceptable is much kinder than to keep it hidden.

In the past, people were reluctant to say that they would not eat certain foods for dietary or religious reasons, in case people thought they were fussy. The social norm has changed so that it is now polite to let your host know before arrival if you cannot eat certain foods. As a host, it is so much easier to know what not to provide, especially if the guest also gives some suggestions as to what they can eat. It saves embarrassment and stress.

We can say what we need to say. We can gently, but assertively, speak our mind. We do not need to be judgmental, tactless, blaming or cruel when we speak our truths.

Melody Beattie

Make the consequences of crossing the boundary clear. Be specific and consistent.

There are times when you need to be forceful and put your own safety first. But there are other times when you care about the person and do not want to hurt their feelings. How can you say no nicely?

SIMPLE to Say No Nicely

Chapters 4 to 7 are full of advice on whether to speak up and how to communicate, so I will just highlight the most important points here. Maintaining boundaries is like saying No nicely; it means you can say Yes to other things. The acronym SIMPLE in Figure 11.2 sums up the art of saying No nicely. You can set boundaries, while still leaving a door that can be opened.

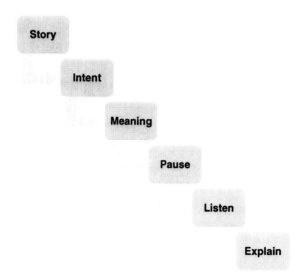

Figure 11.2 SIMPLE The Art of Saying No Nicely

SIMPLE: Tool for Saying No Nicely

Story. Manage your emotions and fears by telling yourself a different story. Instead of imagining rejection or stories of loss, focus on why you want to say No. Be clear about the benefits of saying No, the risks of not speaking up, and how it could improve the relationship. If you have spent some time working out your triggers, this will help, as you will know the reason for saying No. Ask yourself if you really want to say No. Do not delay, if you have made up your mind, tell them. Prepare yourself for their reaction.

Intent. Show your positive intent by respecting the other person. Speak kindly and prepare them for what you are going to say.

Meaning. Do not waffle or skirt the issue. Be honest and as clear as you can, without hurting them unnecessarily. Contrasting can sometimes clarify things. For example, "I like going out with you, but I don't like going to the disco."

Pause. Check they have understood. Give them time to process it. Let them have their say.

Listen. Be empathetic, reminding yourself of the reasons for saying No.

Explain. Sometimes, you need to explain what no means and the consequences. Do not justify or excuse, but stay objective and polite. You may decide that No is the wrong answer, but be wary if this happens too much!

When you have set your boundary, you need to ensure that it is consistently maintained. Do not wait until people have crossed it numerous times. Speak up early. The STAR tool summarizes how to use the skills from this book when someone has crossed a boundary you have set.

STAR Tool

When boundaries are crossed

S. Get your **story straight. Speak up. Start** with something you agree on. **State** what the purpose of the conversation is. **Show** what is in it for them. **Safety** is important. Do not threaten or blame.

(Continued)

T. Take control of your emotions. Be curious, not furious. If you are angry, you will not think straight. **Tell** what you have seen as objectively as possible and how you feel. **Talk tentatively**—do not judge.

A. Admit your part. **Apologize** for your errors. **Ask** for their view of the situation and what they think would solve the issue. **Appreciate** they may see things differently.

R. Resolve: If the solution they suggest is not acceptable, go back to the beginning. **Record the decision:** This need not be a formal document; it could be an e-mail confirming what you decide. This ensures everyone is on the same page, and if the problem recurs, it provides information. **Repeat** if necessary. **Remain** calm and courteous.

Worked example Penny was annoyed that Percy had not paid her bill. Her terms and conditions had been made very clear and he had agreed them beforehand. First, she checked that the goods had been delivered and that the invoice had been issued. Then, she took control of her emotions and rang Percy. "Hi Percy, how are things? Were you happy about the delivery?" Percy, "Yes, it's absolutely super." Penny said, "I'm glad, as I really like working with you and I appreciate that you agreed to pay on delivery. The money doesn't seem to have come through yet—would you like me to send the invoice again?" Percy says, "Oh, I've got the invoice, but I'd like to pay with credit card if I can." Penny doesn't have a credit card, but she knows that it is possible to pay by card through PayPal. "Sure," she says, "I'm sorry I didn't think to put details of how to pay by card and PayPal on the invoice. I'd really appreciate it if you could pay today. I'll send you an e-mail with the details."

Now, Penny has not embarrassed Percy, but has made it clear and easy for him to pay. She has kept a record, so if he does not pay, she has it documented. She may need to repeat the process and talk about consequences if he does not pay. For example, she may have to hold another delivery or even think about legal action. The important thing is for her to keep calm and avoid getting angry.

Conclusion

The aim of this book is to open your eyes to your own potential for managing conflict well. Any small steps you take toward controlling your emotions or understanding others will have a cumulative effect. Conflict is inevitable, but it does not need to cause irreparable damage.

The first key takeaway of this book is that we each have the potential to find a solution. If we blame others for our problems and refuse to acknowledge that we have a choice, we are throwing away control of our own destiny. We need to take responsibility for improving the situation, rather than waiting for others to turn into reasonable people.

The second is that there is no magic method that will solve every problem. There are many tools and theories covered in this book—not all will suit you or be appropriate for every circumstance. We all have different strengths and limitations, and knowing what these are is crucial. Once we have this knowledge, it will help us choose what works the best for each of us. See life as a giant laboratory, and yourself as the scientist. Experiment with different methods, note which work for you and the circumstances. Learn from disasters, repeat successes.

Finally, everyone can improve their ability to control their emotions and to communicate effectively. There is overwhelming scientific evidence of neuroplasticity—the human brain's ability to change and adapt. Scientists no longer believe that IQ and personality traits are fixed at an early age. We can no longer excuse ourselves with phrases such as "I can't help having a short fuse." The better we become at communication, the nicer other people seem to become.

I hope this introduction to conflict first aid has whetted your appetite to learn more, practice the skills, and make life easier for yourself and others.

Check Understanding Chapter 11

- What are the six sources of influence?
- How can focusing on the positive limit the escalation or damage of conflict?

- Why are boundaries important?
- What are two important components of setting boundaries?
- Describe how SIMPLE helps you remember how to say no nicely
- Think of a situation when someone has crossed a boundary and you need to hold them accountable. Explain how you could use the STAR tool to hold them accountable.

CHAPTER 12

Resources

For further study

Conflict

As well as Crucial Conversations (Patterson, Grenny, et al. 2002), Crucial Confrontations (Patterson, Grenny and McMillan, et al. 2005) and Crucial Accountability (Patterson, Grenny, et al. 2013) Kerry Patterson and his team provide a wealth of online resources at https://www.vitalsmarts.com. Two other practical books on conflict resolution are Difficult Conversations (Stone, Patton and Heen 1999) and Disagreements, Disputes and All-out War (Scott 2008). See also the extensive references in the Bibliography.

Listening

Nancy Kline's Time to Think (Kline 1999) and Mark Goulston's Just Listen (Goulston 2010) not only demonstrate the power of listening but also give practical tips.

Mindfulness

The online Beginner's Course offered by Giovanni Dienstmann (Dienstmann n.d.) is an easy way to start. Jon Kabat-Zinn not only wrote the classic book on mindfulness (Kabat-Zinn, Wherever You Go, There You Are 2004), but also created the Mindfulness Based Stress Reduction Programme (Kabat-Zinn 2013).

Trust

Stephen MR Covey's book The Speed of Trust (S. M. Covey 2006)is essential reading for anyone who wants to know more about this fascinating subject. Another excellent book is The Trusted Adviser (Maister, Green and Galford 2002).

Tools

Table of Tools

Some of these tools are also featured in my articles for Business Expert Press Expert Insights Series 2017.

Pause Tool

When something upsetting happens:

Pause and reflect, if only for an instant. You may want to ask for more time.

Ask yourself

Is my instinctive response keeping me safe from physical danger? (If so, let the primitive brain take over. If not, continue)

Take some deep slow breaths. This will calm and strengthen your heart beat and clear your mind.

Notice how you feel

Ask yourself

What actually happened?

What did I tell myself it meant?

What is another explanation for what happened?

Choose how you want to react.

Posture for Confidence

For the Brave: Wonder Woman Pose. Find somewhere unobserved and stand straight, shoulders back, hands on hips and legs apart for two minutes. (When I demonstrated this to school staff, they said "Ah, the teacher pose.") If done when others are around, it may be seen as arrogant or threatening, so use with caution.

For the Not So Brave: Straighten Sit up straight, rest your hands open on your knees or desk, uncross your legs and put feet firmly on the ground. Tilting your head slightly forward deepens and slows your voice. Simon Raybould produced a series of videos (Raybould 2015), demonstrating different postures which make you look and feel more confident.

The Position of Joy

Sit comfortably with your feet touching the floor and your spine straight.

Rest your hands on your thighs with your palms pointing upwards and your fingers gently curved.

Relax your shoulders.

Raise your head.

Take a few slow, deep breaths.

Let go of your anger and fear.

Bessel van der Kolk describes this as a position in which it is impossible to be angry. (Kolk 2017)

Posture for Soothing 1: Settling the Body

Sit comfortably with your feet touching the floor and your spine straight.

Put your right hand under your left armpit, with your palm facing inwards beside your heart.

Wrap your left arm around the front of your body so that your left palm touches your upper right arm or shoulder.

Hold yourself gently and firmly in this position, breathing slowly and deeply.

Be aware of the sensation, not just of your hands, but also of your inner body sensations.

Most people report a feeling of settling and safety.

Breathe slowly and deeply, until you feel more settled and calm.

Posture for Soothing 2: Settling the Mind and Body

Sit comfortably with your feet touching the floor and your spine straight.

Place the palm of one hand on your forehead, and the palm of your other had on your upper chest.

This can be done with eyes open or closed, whichever must

(Continued)

Breathe slowly and deeply, noticing the sensations of your hands and in your head between your hands.

Leave your hands there until you feel some shift or flow.

Once you feel this, leaving the lower hand on your chest, move the upper hand to your belly.

Breathe slowly and deeply, noticing the sensations in your body between your hands.

Sad to Glad Tool

How to change your perspective on mishaps and mistakes

G: What **good** can you see? What can you be **grateful** for? **Guess** what benefit it might bring

L: What can you **learn** from this situation? What can you **laugh** about? Is there anything **lucky**?

A: What **action** would make the situation better? **Acknowledge** your part. **Ask** what now? **Ask for help** if needed.

D: Decide not to let this ruin your day. **Distract** yourself. **Distance** yourself.

This works for most things, but start with something small first.

Worked example For example, I have dropped a bottle of milk, spilling it over the floor.

G: It's good I have plenty of milk. Grateful it didn't go on my clothes, I guess someone might help me clean it up and save me having to wash the floor this evening.

L: I've learned that I should watch where I put the milk and not to try and do 2 things at once. I'm laughing at myself treating spilled milk as an exercise. It's lucky I have plenty of time this morning.

A: Instead of feeling bad, I can clean up. Or I could ask someone to help. I'm aware it was my fault.

D: Well, it won't ruin my day. I'll just forget about it now and get on with having a great day.

Bystander Tool

Think of a recent occasion when you were angry or frightened.

Bystander's View:

Give a report of the event as though you were observing it as a bystander, NOT from your point of view. Be as objective, accurate and clear as possible, no explanations, justifications or reasons.

Write an objective description of the event

OR draw a comic strip of the event.

OR tell it out loud

Don't worry about your speaking, writing or drawing skills, just what happened. Have a break of at least an hour before you move on.

Your View:

Describe what emotions and thoughts you had at each point as though you were speaking to the observer, as objectively and clearly as you can. You need to make sure a stranger would understand your reasoning and your reaction. You may find it helpful to sit in one chair as participant and another as speaker. Imagine the bystander saying, "What made you think that? What did you think was going to happen? What previous experience did it recall?"

For example:

You were angry because someone was late. Did that cause a problem like missing a train? Or is it because they rarely arrive on time and you want to change the pattern? Or does their lateness makes you think that they do not respect or care for you? Or were you hungry or tired or upset about something else? What thoughts were going through your mind?

SCIM Tool: Deciding to Speak Up or Not

This helps you remember the key factors to consider when you are wondering whether to speak up.

S: Is it **safe**? Is it **sensible** to speak up now or will it be wise to wait?

C: What are the **consequences** if I don't speak up? What does my **conscience** say? What do I need to **consider**?

I: What is **important**? Do I have all the **information** I need?

M: What is my **motive** in speaking out? What skills do I need to make my **meaning** clear? Is this the best **method** to improve the situation?

ABC When Trust is Broken

Like a hand knitted sweater, trust takes many actions to create, but a single snag can unravel the whole garment. The sooner you act to stop the damage the better.

A: Acknowledge that something is wrong. **Admit** your part. **Apologise** for any action that hurt the other. **Ask** what you can do to put things right. **Accept** that the other may not be ready to heal or forgive. **Act** as though you can be trusted.

B: Believe the other acted from an unsatisfied need. **Behave** as though you want to repair the relationship. **Build** on common values.

C: Care for the other. Be **consistent**. **Clarify** your intentions. Have **compassion** for yourself and the other involved. **Choose** your path wisely.

Risk Assessment Tool

If I do nothing			
Positive Consequence	Chance of this	Negative Consequence	Chance of this
If I intervene			
Positive Consequence	Chance of this	Negative Consequence	Chance of this

TRIP UP Assessment Tool

An exercise to check whether you should intervene in others' conflicts

Time: Is this the right time and place to intervene? Is there a need for immediate action? Is it a good idea to act now? Can it wait?

Risks: What are the consequences of doing nothing? What are the chances that there will be negative outcomes from intervening?

Intent: What do I hope to achieve by intervening? What is the ideal outcome? What is the worst thing that could happen? Will my intent be reflected in my action (lack of action)?

Personality: Do the people involved have any specific issues/sensitivities? What will help them find resolution? What are their triggers? Am I the right person to handle this conflict or is someone else better suited?

Understanding: Do I know what is happening? Do I need more information? Is there someone else who might know more?

P: Problem: What is the cause of the problem? What has triggered the issue? It is the behaviour, the pattern or the relationship that needs fixing?

(Continued)

Worked example For example, in the toilets of Multiple Manufacturing, manager Jim overhears recent recruit Fred moaning to a colleague that he wasn't invited to join his teammates for a drink the Friday before, so he is not going to volunteer or do anything he doesn't have to.

> **T:** It is something that could impact on work, so probably needs to be dealt with sooner than later. Toilets aren't really the place to have a private conversation.
>
> **R:** There is a risk that if nothing is done, Fred will affect productivity or there will be conflict within the team. The manager was not supposed to hear what Fred said, so bringing it up with Fred or his team leader overtly might make Fred angry. The team might be angry if they feel the manager is dictating to them about their social life.
>
> **I:** Jim doesn't want to cause more problems. He doesn't want to micromanage or undermine the team leader. He wants Fred to work well with the team.
>
> **P:** Jim knows the team leader well. He is a sensible chap and Jim has a chat with each team manager once a day for five or ten minutes.
>
> **U:** Jim doesn't know what Fred is like and thinks it might be helpful to know more about the situation before trying to fix things.
>
> **P:** Jim is not sure whether it is just the lack of invitation, a pattern or a breakdown in the relationship.

What Jim did

Having considered the various factors, Jim had a chat with Paul, the team manager, asking how Fred had settled in to the team. Paul said that things had gone pretty well, but this week, Fred seemed to be very off hand and he didn't know why. Jim asked if there had been any incidents. Paul couldn't think. So, Jim asked if the team socialised much after work. "Oh, yeah", says Paul "we go out every Friday after work". Jim asked if Fred joined in. After the first week, everyone assumed that Fred would just come along, but he didn't. Jim's approach made Paul realise that perhaps Fred felt he had to wait to be invited. Later that

(Continued)

day, Paul said casually to Fred that he was sorry Fred hadn't joined them on Friday. Paul said, "After the first week, we don't ask people to come just in case they feel embarrassed to say no. Any time you want to come, just come along. Whether it's just once or twice a year, or never, it doesn't make any difference." Fred's attitude brightened up, and a low-key response averted problems.

SALAD Tool

How to react when anger is in charge . . .

S. Safety First ensure you are safe. When others become angry, especially if drink or drugs are involved, violence can burst out. If you don't feel safe, leave. **Switch off your anger**, switch on logic. Keep calm. Take a few deep breaths and remind yourself that there is a reason why the person is angry. Think of the best outcome for this conversation. Keep **silent** to give yourself time to manage your emotions.

A. Acknowledge the person's emotion and **ask** them for their view of the situation. Don't say "Why are you angry"—they may not know and they may see this as you saying they should not be. Instead **ask** them to tell you more about how they feel and what has happened from their point of view.

L. Listen. Let them talk until they stop, then ask if there is anything more. Paraphrase what they have said and check understanding. Help them put words to their emotions and gradually gain control so they can thing **logically.**

A. Ask what would make them feel better. **Acknowledge** their right to feel the way they do, even if you don't agree. **Agree** what you can.

D.Do what you can. Don't promise things you can't deliver. **Deliver** on any promises you make. Follow up. **Decide** together what is the next step and if necessary **document** it.

Responsibility Pie Chart Tool

Negative events are due to a combination of three types of factors: our own actions, the actions of others and random unpredictable things.

Start by thinking of a negative event that happened to you recently.

Fill in the first a pie chart illustrating the three factors without thinking.

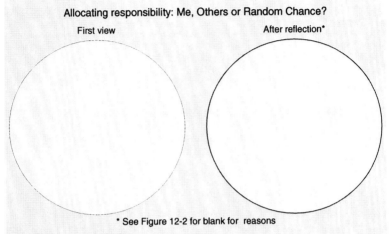

Allocating responsibility: Me, Others or Random Chance?

First view   After reflection*

* See Figure 12-2 for blank for reasons

Figure 12.1 Blank Pie Charts

Now, list all the reasons that contributed to the result. Try and put down everything that contributed to the event, however small.

Reason for event	percentage	Category (Me/Other/Chance

Figure 12.2 Blank for Reasons (RPC Tool)

(Continued)

(see the worked example below for further guidance on how to use this tool). You must always allocate some responsibility to yourself, as you chose to be there. It is useful to try and avoid the words 'blame' and 'fault'

- How much was . . . responsible for what happened?
- How much was what happened due to . . .?
- How much did this happen because of . . .?
- How much does . . . explain what happened?

Starting with the least important factor, give each factor a percentage and group them into the three categories mentioned above.

Add up the categories and draw your pie chart again.

Compare the two.

What can you learn about yourself from the way you apportion responsibility?

What would you do differently next time?

Worked Example

Mary and Dennis were business partners in a bakery as well as spouses. Mary managed the bakers and Dennis ran the retail shop. One day, the flour delivery was late, so not all the varieties of loaves were ready, despite the bakers rushing like mad to try and get things done. They were so busy baking that Mary had not told Dennis why they were late. When a customer complained that her favourite loaf was not ready, Dennis said "So sorry, I'll be remonstrating with the bakers about their idleness." Mary overheard this and was furious. When Dennis came back into the oven room, she snapped "You are one to talk about idleness. You just get to chat away to the customers. We're the ones who have to rush around doing all the work. You get all the praise and blame us when things go wrong. You have no idea of the problems we solve while you sit out there chatting." Dennis thought she was overreacting and told her so, defending himself and maintaining that if it wasn't for his sales ability there wouldn't be a business . . .things went downhill from there.

(Continued)

The two pie charts below show the change in Mary's thinking. Initially she thought that she had little responsibility for the argument, blaming it on mainly on Dennis. When she asked herself the objective questions, she realised the role that chance had played in the customer coming in when they had, the reason for the delivery being late and her own responsibility for letting Dennis know what was happening and losing her temper.

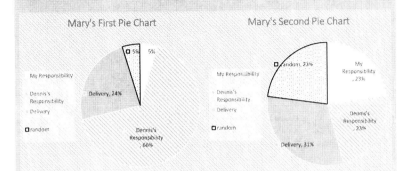

Figure 12.3 Worked Example of Pie Chart Exercise

Do you think this altered perspective would have helped Mary find other ways to recover from the situation? Does recognising your responsibility in a negative situation provide new ideas on how to improve or resolve the situation?

SEAM Apology Tool

For an apology to be effective, it must come from the heart and be sincere. The sooner an apology is offered, the better. If the person is very hurt or angry, you may have to offer the apology more than once. The longer you leave the less effective it will be and the harder it will be to apologise. No matter how good an actor you are, if you are defensive or angry, your tone and body language will betray you. So not only do you need to get the words right, you need to get the feelings right. SEAM reminds us of what makes a good apology that will help stitch relationships back together.

(Continued)

- **Seek perspective** Try and see the situation from the other person's point of view. How would your actions have seemed? What are the benefits of restoring your relationship with this person? What have you lost by damaging the relationship? Think about the person's characteristics that attract you and the good things they have done for you. Don't try and justify your actions. Be clear about your motives.

- **Express remorse.** An apology is not a justification of your actions. Start with "I'm sorry I . . . (insert action or behaviour). I feel ashamed of myself." A real apology acknowledges the validity of the feelings or values of the other person. Saying "I'm sorry you were upset by my comment. It was just a joke" implies that the other person can't take a joke. It would be better to say "I'm sorry you were upset by my comment. I should have realised it could be hurtful."

- **Admit responsibility.** Taking responsibility means not only admitting that your behaviour was wrong but also showing that you understand the implications of the behaviour. Don't offer excuses or reasons for your behaviour until the other person asks for them.

    Imagine you are angry for sitting waiting in a bar for a partner to turn up. Compare "Sorry I'm late for our date, but I got held up in traffic" with "I'm so sorry I'm late. I feel bad that you had to wait so long for me. I really wanted to be here on time so we could have lots of time together. I should have allowed more time for traffic on a Friday."

- **Make amends.** The most wonderful apology is meaningless if you don't offer to make amends, and you don't follow through. The other person needs to be reassured that you have recognised the error of your ways, you want to put things right and that you won't do it again. Ask what you can do and follow through. Don't make promises you can't keep. Explain how you plan to change your behaviour in the future. The follow through is essential. The more you keep your word, the more effective your apologies will be.

Forgiveness Tool 1 Letters

Write a letter to the person who hurt you (which you are not going to send), recalling the incident, telling them of the impact it had on you. Pour your heart out.

Now imagine how you would like that person to respond to your hurt. Write a letter as though the other person was responding to your pain with understanding and empathy. Describe the possible reasons behind the behaviour. Say what could be done to ease your pain. Write of the problems from the other person's point of view.

Now read the letter. Allow yourself to feel compassion and understanding and write back describing what you feel and what forgiveness means to you.

Remind yourself that forgiveness is your choice and your gift. Think of the peace it will bring you and the benefits.

Now burn all the letters.

If you have decided to forgive, write a reminder to do something that will show your forgiveness. If you have not decided to forgive, you may find talking to an impartial third party helpful.

Forgiveness Tool 2 Chairs

Find a private place and set up three chairs.

Imagine the person who wronged you is sitting in the other chair. Speak to him/her honestly and clearly about the impact of his/her behaviour on you. Tell them how you feel, what hurts most and what you would like them to do. Once you have poured out your heart and expressed all your emotions, take a deep breath.

Change chairs. Now imagine you are the other person and there is an imaginary you are sitting opposite. Talk back to the imaginary you in a way that helps you see why the other person might have behaved the way he/she did. What could make people behave that way? What need might have been driving the behaviour?

(Continued)

Pause, breathe and change chairs so that you are sitting in the third chair. Try and see the situation as an impartial third party. Help reconcile the two views. Ask what next?

If you have decided to forgive, write a reminder to do something that will show your forgiveness.

If you cannot forgive, you may find talking to an expert third party helps you to move on.

Influencer Tool

Area	Motivation	Ability
Personal	I want to do it.	I am able to do it
Social	My family and friends want me to do it.	My friends and family help me do it
Structural	My environment/the law encourages me to do it.	My environment/the law enables me to do it.

Figure 12-4 Sources of Influence (from Influencer, 2008)

Choose a specific instance of resistant (or wrong in your eyes) behaviour. Answering the questions below will help you find reasons for the resistant behaviour and give you insights into what (if anything) can be done to change others' behaviour. You may reassess your views on the behaviour. Work through the model and ask yourself the questions.

Source 1 Personal Motivation: Do they want to engage in the behaviour? Do they enjoy it? What would make them want to behave in the desired way?

Source 2 – Personal Ability – Do they know the consequences and benefits? Do they have the skills needed to behave in the desired way? What strengths do they have? What do they need?

(Continued)

Source 3 – **Social Motivation** – Are other people encouraging the right behaviour and discouraging the wrong behaviour? What could be done to create positive peer pressure?

Source 4 – Social Ability – Are friends able to provide the help, information, and/or resources required? What can family or other social groups provide?

Source 5 – Structural Motivation – Are rewards, pay, promotions, performance reviews, perks, or costs encouraging the right behaviours? Does the unwanted behaviour incur any penalty or negative consequence?

Source 6 – Structural Ability – Are there enough cues to stay on course? Does the environment (tools, facilities, information, reports, proximity to others, policies) enable the right behaviour? What might make it harder to do the wrong thing?

What ideas has this given you? Has it changed your views in any way?

Rose Tinted Glasses Tool

Think of the parties in the conflict in terms of their work, their personalities and their contribution.

- Describe a good time that you had with the other person, or something that they did which helped you, or a contribution that you valued.
- Remember something that you did for them that made you feel good. Was there an achievement that you did with them that you are proud of?
- What do you (did you) particularly value about the person or the relationship? What benefits did the relationship bring you? What were the key factors in the relationship?
- What three wishes do you have for the relationship going forward? What could you do to bring them into existence?

SIMPLE: Tool for Saying No Nicely

Story. Manage your emotions and fears by telling yourself a different story. Instead of imagining rejection or stories of loss, focus on why you want to say no. Be clear about the benefits of saying no, the risks of not speaking up and how it could improve the relationship. If you have spent some time working out your triggers, this will help, as you will know the reason for saying no. Ask yourself if you really want to say no. Don't delay, if you've made up your mind, tell them. Prepare yourself for their reaction.

Intent. Show your positive intent by respecting the other person. Speak kindly and prepare them for what you are going to say.

Meaning. Don't waffle or skirt the issue. Be honest and as clear as you can, without hurting them unnecessarily. Contrasting can sometimes clarify things. For example," I like going out with you, but I don't like going to the disco."

Pause. Check they've understood. Give them time to process it. Let them have their say.

Listen. Be empathetic, reminding yourself of the reasons for saying no.

Explain. Sometimes, you need to explain what no means and the consequences. Don't justify or excuse, but stay objective and polite. You may decide that no is the wrong answer, but be wary if this happens too much!

STAR Tool
When boundaries are crossed

S. Get your **story straight. Speak up. Start** with something you agree on. **State** what the purpose of the conversation is. **Show** what's in it for them. **Safety** is important. Don't threaten or blame.

T. Take control of your emotions. Be curious, not furious. If you are angry, you will not think straight. **Tell** what you have seen

(Continued)

as objectively as possible and how you feel. **Talk tentatively—** don't judge.

A. **Admit** your part. **Apologize** for your errors. **Ask** for their view of the situation and what they think would solve the issue. **Appreciate** they may see things differently.

R. **Resolve:** If the solution they suggest is not acceptable, go back to the beginning. **Record the decision:** This need not be a formal document; it could be an e-mail confirming what you decide. This ensures everyone is on the same page, and if the problem recurs, it provides information. **Repeat** if necessary. **Remain** calm and courteous.

Worked example

Penny was annoyed that Percy had not paid her bill. Her terms and conditions had been made very clear and he had agreed them beforehand. First, she checked that the goods had been delivered and that the invoice had been issued. Then she took control of her emotions and rang Percy. "Hi Percy, how are things? Were you happy about the delivery?" Percy, "Yes, it's absolutely super." Penny said, "I'm glad, as I really like working with you and I appreciate that you agreed to pay on delivery. The money doesn't seem to have come through yet—would you like me to send the invoice again?" Percy says, "Oh, I've got the invoice, but I'd like to pay with credit card if I can." Penny doesn't have a credit card, but she knows that it is possible to pay by card through PayPal. "Sure," she says, "I'm sorry I didn't think to put details of how to pay by card and PayPal on the invoice. I'd really appreciate it if you could pay today. I'll send you an email with the details."

Now, Penny has not embarrassed Percy, but has made it clear and easy for him to pay. She's kept a record, so if he doesn't pay, she has it documented. She may need to repeat the process and talk about consequences if he doesn't pay. For example, she may have to hold another delivery or even think about legal action. The important thing is for her to keep calm and avoid getting angry.

References

Adams, M. 2012. "What are the Essential Components of an I-Message." *Gordon Training International.* 31 May. Accessed June 22, 2017. http://www.gordontraining.com/leadership/what-are-the-essential -components-of-an-i-message/#.

Asch, S. E. 1951. "Effects of group pressure upon the modification and distortion of judgment." In *Groups, leadership and men.*, by H. Guetzkow (ed.). Pittsburgh, PA: Carnegie Press.

Berg, Yehuda *The Power of Words* November 17 2011 http://www.huffing-tonpost.com/yehuda-berg/the-power-of-words_1_b_716183.html Accessed

Bruneau, Emile G, and Rebecca Saxe. 2012. "Conflict, The power of being heard: The benefits of 'perspective-giving' in the context of intergroup." *Journal of Experimental Social Psychology*, 2 March: 855-856.

Carney, Dana. 2015. "My position on "Power Poses"." *www.berkeley.edu.* Accessed May 23, 2017. http://faculty.haas.berkeley.edu/dana_carney/pdf_My%20position%20on%20power%20poses.pdf.

Carney, Dana R, Amy J.C Cuddy, and Andy J Yap. 2010. "Power Posing: Brief Nonverbal Displays Affect Neuroendocrine Levels and Risk Tolerance." *Association for Psychological Science* 1363-1368.

Center for NonViolent Communication. 2008. "NVC Instruction Guide." *Center for Nonviolent Communication.* 5 8. http://www.cnvc .org/online-learning/nvc-instruction-guide/nvc-instruction-guide.

Cooperrider, D. L., Whitney, D., & Stavros, J. M. 2003. *Appreciative inquiry handbook.* Bedford Heights, OH: Lakeshore Publishers.

Covey, Stephen M.R. 2006. *The Speed of Trust.* New York: Simon & Schuster.

Covey, Stephen R. 2004. *Seven Habits of Highly Effective People.* Sydney: Simon & Schuster.

CPP Global Human Capital Report. July 2008. *Workplace Conflict and How Businesses can Harness it to Thrive.* Mountain View: CPP Global.

Cuddy, Amy. 2012. *Your Body Language Shapes Who You Are.* 1 October. https://youtu.be/Ks-_Mh1QhMc/.

Dana, Daniel. 2001. *Conflict Resolution: Mediation Tools for Everyday Life.* New York: McGraw Hill.

Dienstmann, Giovanni. n.d. *Live and Dare.* Accessed June 5, 2017. http://bit.ly/2bSAFEY.

Frankl, Victor. 1962. *Man's Search for Meaning.* London: Rider.

Gorlick, Adam. 2014. "Media multitaskers pay mental price, Stanford study shows." *Stanford University.* 24 August. Accessed June 2, 2017. http://news.stanford.edu/2009/08/24/multitask-research-study-082409/.

Goulston, Mark. 2010. *Just Listen.* New York: Amacom. n.d. *Greater Good Berkeley Forgiveness.* Accessed July 3, 2017. https://greatergood.berkeley.edu/forgiveness/definition.

Grenny, Joseph How to Address Bad Body Odour May 30 2017 https://www.vitalsmarts.com/crucialskills/2017/05/how-to-address-bad-body-odor/

Grenny, Joseph, and David Maxfield. 2015. *One Simple Skill to Overcome Peer Pressure | The Behavioral Science Guys.* 2 March. Accessed May 31, 2017. https://www.youtube.com/watch?v=1-U6QTRTZSc.

Hardesty, Larry. 2010. "Social Studies." *MIT Technology Review.* 27 October. Accessed June 20, 2017. https://www.technologyreview.com/s/421386/social-studies/ n.d. *International Association of Mediators.* http://www.iamed.org/member/JohnSturrock.

John Ford & Associates. 2007. *How Much is Conflict Costing You? .* Oakland, California: : John Ford and Associates. .

Kabat-Zinn, Jon. 2013. *Full catastrophe living (revised edition): using the wisdom of your body and mind to face stress, pain, and illness.* Bantam. 2004. *Wherever You Go, There You Are.* Piatkus: London.

Kline, Nancy. 1999. *Time to Think.* London: Ward Lock.

Kolk, Bessel van der. 2017. *Demonstrating the Position of Joy.* 6 March. https://youtu.be/8-pBcF3FvQM.

Lenski, Tammy. n.d. "5 uncomplicated ways to gain psychological distance during conflict (and why you should)." *Tammy Lenski.* Accessed May 31, 2017. https://lenski.com/psychological-distance/.

Levine, Peter. 2017. *Two Simple Techniques that can Help Trauma Patients Feel Safe.* 2 June. Accessed June 11, 2017. https://youtu.be/G7zAseaIyFA.

Maister, David, Charles H Green, and Robert Galford. 2002. *Trusted Advisor.* New York: Simon Schuster.

Moore, Christopher. 2003. *The Mediation Process.* San Francisco: Jossey Bass.

Morris, David Z. 2016. *Power Poses' Researcher Dana Carney Now Says Effects are "Undeniably" False.* 2 October. Accessed May 22, 2017. http://fortune.com/2016/10/02/power-poses-research-false/.

Noble, Toni, and Helen McGrath. 2008. "The positive educational practices framework: A tool for facilitating the work of educational psychologists." *Educational & Child Psychology,* No 2 Vol 25 : 119-134.

Ohlin, Birgit. 2016. "Active Listening." *Positive Psychology Program.* 21 July. Accessed 6 2, 2017. https://positivepsychologyprogram.com/active-listening/.

Ohno, Taiichi. 2006. *Toyota Traditions.* March. Accessed June 16, 2017. http://www.toyota-global.com/company/toyota_traditions/quality/mar_apr_2006.html.

Patterson, Kerry, Joseph Grenny, David Maxfield, Ron Macmillan, and Ron Switzler. 2008. *Influencer: The Power to Change Anything.* New York: McGraw Hill.

Patterson, Kerry, Joseph Grenny, David Maxfield, Ron McMillan, and Al Switzler. 2011. *Change Anything.* London: Piatkus.

———2013. *Crucial Accountability: Tools for Resolving Violated Expectations, Broken Commitments & Bad Behaviour.* New York: McGraw-Hill.

———2002. *Crucial Conversations: Tools for Talking When Stakes are High.* New York: McGraw-Hill.

Patterson, Kerry, Joseph Grenny, Ron McMillan, and Al Switzler. 2005. *Crucial Confrontations.* New York: McGraw Hill.

Peters, Steve. 2011. *The Chimp Paradox.* London: Vermilion.

Peterson, Christopher. 2006. *Primer of Positive Psychology.* Oxford: Oxford University Press.

Ranehill, Eve, Anna Dreber, Magnus Johannesson, Susanne Leiberg, Sunhae Sul, and Roberto Weber. 2015. "Assessing the Robustness of Power Posing: No Effect on Hormones and Risk Tolerance in a Large Sample of Men and Women." *Association for Psychological Science* 1-4.

Rath, Tom, and Donald 0. Clifton. 2004. *How Full is Your Bucket: Positive Strategies for Work and Life.* New York: Gallup.

Raybould, Simon. 2015. *Power of Peripheral Vision Managing.* 18 July. Accessed May 22, 2017. https://youtu.be/UMqexD_oz0c.

———2015. *Managing Pressure Situations Simon Raybould.* 19 July. Accessed May 22, 2017. https://www.youtube.com/watch?v=j78pG1R2fGg.

——— 2015. *Power of Posture: Managing Pressure Situations.* 18 July. Accessed May 22, 2017. https://youtu.be/eZBFmeBM1ao.

Rock, David. 2009. *Your Brain at Work.* New York: Harper Collins.

Rosenberg, Marshall B. 2015. *Non Violent Communication: A Language of Life.* Alberqueque: Puddledancer Press.

Scheier, Michael F, and Charles S Carver. 1985. "Optimism, coping and health: Assessment and implications of generalised outcome expectancies." *Health Psychology Vol 4 (3)* 219-247.

Scott, Gina Graham. 2008. *Disagreements, Disputes and All-Out War.* New York: AMACOM.

2005. "Silence Kills." *Vital Smarts.* Accessed May 4, 2017. https://www.vitalsmarts.com/resource/silent-treatment/.

Stone, Douglas, Bruce Patton, and Sheila Heen. 1999. *Difficult Conversations:How to Discuss What Matters Most.* London: Penguin.

Swee, Genevieve, and Annett Schimer. 2015. "On the Importance of Being Vocal: Saying "Ow" Improves Pain Tolerance." *The Journal of Pain*, April: 326-334.

Taylor, Jill Bolte. 2006. *Stroke of Insight: A Brain Scientist's Personal Journey.* New York: Viking.

Toussaint, L.L, A.D Owen, and A Cheadle. 2012. "Forgive to Live: Forgiveness, health and longevity. ." *Journal of Behavioural Medicine* 375-386.

Ury, William. 1991. *Getting Past No.* London: Business Books.

Ury, Willliam. 2010. "Walk from No to Yes." *TED Talks.* October. Accessed June 26 2017. https://www.ted.com/talks/william_ury/transcript?language=en.

VIA Institute on Character. n.d. *The VIA Survey.* Accessed May 31, 2017. https://www.viacharacter.org/www/Character-Strengths-Survey.

Wiseman, Richard. 2012. *Rip it up.* London: Macmillan.

———2003. *The Luck Factor.* London: Century.

Wolpert, Stuart. 2007. "Putting Feelings Into Words Produces Therapeutic Effects in the Brain." *UCL Newsroom*. 21 June. Accessed June 21, 2017. http://newsroom.ucla.edu/releases/ Putting-Feelings-Into-Words-Produces-8047.

Worthington, Everett. 2016. *Everett Worthington Forgiveness*. Accessed July 3, 2017. http://www.evworthington-forgiveness.com/reach-forgiveness -of-others/.

Index

OTHER TITLES IN THE HUMAN RESOURCE MANAGEMENT AND ORGANIZATIONAL BEHAVIOR COLLECTION

- *Slow Down to Speed Up: Lead, Succeed, and Thrive in a 24/7 World* by Liz Bywater
- *Temperatism, Volume I: A New Way to Think About Business and Doing Good* by Carrie Foster
- *The DNA of Leadership: Creating Healthy Leaders and Vibrant Organizations* by Myron Beard and Alan Weiss
- *How to Manage Your Career: The Power of Mindset in Fostering Success* by Kelly Swingler
- *21st Century Skills for Non-Profit Managers: A Practical Guide on Leadership and Management* by Don Macdonald, Charles Oham, and Sue Causton
- *Infectious Innovation: Secrets of Transforming Employee Ideas into Dramatic Revenue Growth* by James Allan
- *Agile Human Resources: Creating a Sustainable Future for the HR Profession* by Kelly Swingler
- *Deconstructing Management Maxims, Volume I: A Critical Examination of Conventional Business Wisdom* by Kevin Wayne
- *Deconstructing Management Maxims, Volume II: A Critical Examination of Conventional Business Wisdom* by Kevin Wayne
- *The Real Me: Find and Express Your Authentic Self* by Mark Eyre
- *Across the Spectrum: What Color Are You?* by Stephen Elkins-Jarrett
- *Life of a Lifetime: Inspiration for Creating Your Extraordinary Life* by Christoph Spiessens
- *The Facilitative Leader: Managing Performance Without Controlling People* by Steve Reilly
- *The Human Resource Professional's Guide to Change Management: Practical Tools and Techniques to Enact Meaningful and Lasting Organizational Change* by Melanie J. Peacock
- *Tough Calls: How to Move Beyond Indecision and Good Intentions* by Linda D. Henman
- *Human Resources as Business Partner: How to Maximize The Value and Financial Contribution of HR* by Tony Miller
- *The Challenge to Be and Not to Do: How to Manage Your Career and Maximize Your Potential* by Carrie Foster

Announcing the Business Expert Press Digital Library

Concise e-books business students need for classroom and research

This book can also be purchased in an e-book collection by your library as

- *a one-time purchase,*
- *that is owned forever,*
- *allows for simultaneous readers,*
- *has no restrictions on printing, and*
- *can be downloaded as PDFs from within the library community.*

Our digital library collections are a great solution to beat the rising cost of textbooks. E-books can be loaded into their course management systems or onto students' e-book readers. The **Business Expert Press** digital libraries are very affordable, with no obligation to buy in future years. For more information, please visit **www.businessexpertpress.com/librarians**. To set up a trial in the United States, please email **sales@businessexpertpress.com**.